HALT! DISMOUNT AND BE RECOGNIZED

"Exploring the collision of everyday life and an incredible God"

-JASON CARR-

Copyright © 2008 by Jason Carr

Halt! Dismount And Be Recognized
"Exploring the collision of everyday life and an incredible God"
by Jason Carr

Printed in the United States of America

ISBN 978-1-60647-498-3

All rights reserved solely by the author. The author guarantees all contents are original and do not infringe upon the legal rights of any other person or work. No part of this book may be reproduced in any form without the permission of the author. The views expressed in this book are not necessarily those of the publisher.

Unless otherwise indicated, Bible quotations are taken from The New International Version of the Bible, Copyright © 1984 by Zondervan Publishers, and The Message Bible, Copyright © 2002 by NavPress Publishing Group.

www.xulonpress.com

Thanks for Reading! Enjoy the Journey!

[signature]

John 16:33

THANKS for Reading!

Enjoy the Journey!

John 16:33

Table of Contents

INTRODUCTION

Dedication ix
Getting Started xi
What's Up With The Title? xv

HALT!

HALT — Intro 17
A Lot of Noise 19
Be Still 22
Like A Deer 25
Did You Say Something? 27
Making it Personal 30
Dig Deeper 34

DISMOUNT

DISMOUNT — Intro 37
From the Back Porch 39
A Dog's Life 41
A Long Day in November 44
Remodel 49
Dig Deeper 52

That Night in Alabama 54
Supergroup 57
Ladies and Gentleman…An Idiot! 60
PK 64
Do I Get a Choice Here? 67
Dig Deeper 70

Like Haitian Vanilla? 72
Get Help! 75
Hitch…As a Large Balding White Guy 77
Will the Real Jason Carr Stand Up? 79
The Big C 82
Dig Deeper 85

The Greatest Ending Ever! 87
And the Winner Is… 90
I Hate the Mirror 92
Living Blind 96
Thoughts From an Airplane 98
Dig Deeper 101

The Dentist 103
Life as a Coffee Snob 105
That Kid 109
The Humbling Fields 113
Time to Move On 117
Dig Deeper 121

BE RECOGNIZED

BE RECOGNIZED — Intro 125
Mixed Messages 127
Pieces of Me 130
Fed Up? 133
The Greatest Recognition Ever 136
The End 140
Dig Deeper 142

{thank YOU} 145
About the Author 149

HALT! DISMOUNT AND BE RECOGNIZED

"Exploring the collision of everyday life and an incredible God"

This book is dedicated to the guys that I've had the privilege of leading in small group over the years. May every word remind you of how amazing our God is. I know this to be true; what you are holding is because of the collision of our journeys and our amazing God. Thank you for giving me the chance to be on the journey with you…your lives have changed mine!

HALT! DISMOUNT AND BE RECOGNIZED

Getting Started

Hey there! How are ya? I know, that's not good grammar, but hey we're friends here, right? What you're holding in your hands is something very important to me. If you don't know me, I'm not necessarily the guy you would vote as "Most Likely To Write a Book." In fact, I'd likely make the list of "People Who Would Never Write a Book." Well, here it is, so how 'bout that!?!

I'm a simple person. I grew up in (what was then) a small town, I have great parents who love me and still love each other after 30+ years. For the majority of my adult life I've had the pleasure of working in the same town I am from. Most of that time has been spent in student ministry, mostly hanging out and speaking to students about growing a deeper relationship with God.

This book has been written all over the place—seriously. It has been written in planes, hotel rooms, cabins, back porches, coffee shops, and even sitting in the passenger seat of my car heading to a retreat. I don't write that to make myself sound cool, I write that to tell you that it has taken quite a while to get to the point where you are holding this nifty little book in your hand. God has been brewing the message of this book up over the last season of my life and I am very, very excited to be able to share it with you. I want you to know that I believe you're reading this for a reason. I don't think that God makes mistakes, so there is a reason He brought this book into your life. It's not that my writing or my words are all that—but He is. And I am praying that He uses this book to challenge and encourage you on your life's journey.

To get started, here is something I wrote last spring when I was in Orlando at Disney World "chaperoning" a trip for a friend's group. (I say "chaperoning" because I think I had more fun than the students did.)

* * * * * * *

A little while ago I was strapped into Space Mountain at Disney World…just waiting. I stood in line for quite a while and I couldn't wait to go on what is no doubt one of my favorite roller coasters. It was awesome when I was a kid and it still is awesome!

Let me mention this to you: I am quite a big and tall man. Roller coasters are not the most comfortable things in the world for me. I wonder what it would be like to ride one if I were a super-skinny person—would I be flopping around everywhere?

Have you ever thought about the fact that we all have different experiences on the same ride? One person might be deathly afraid of a ride and another can't wait to ride it again and again. One person might be really uncomfortable and another doesn't even think about it. The same is true in life; we all have different experiences while we're on the same ride.

* * * * * * *

As you read this book you'll find out a bit about what the ride of my life has looked liked so far. My journey is nothing special. I hope I am not so proud to think that my life is so cool that you need to know me. In fact it's quite the opposite. I've messed up so much it still amazes me that God still loves me and even wants to use me. The same is true for you. I've learned that the collision between my everyday life and an incredible God is quite a mess. But because God can make good out of everything- it is a beautiful mess!

Here is the lowdown on this book: You can read it on your own or in a group. I actually want to encourage you to grab a few friends and read it together. At the end of each section will be a page called "Dig Deeper." On this page there are some questions to help you chew on what you've read a little more. There are also some verses you can check out and some suggested songs that connect with the different things you'll read about. All that is there to help you dig in a little deeper and really think about what you've read. I once heard my pastor say, "Hearing a talk is like driving a nail in the wall. If you only tap the nail in, it won't hold much. It's when you really dig in and get the nail driven in that it can really hold something." I think the same is true when we read or think about something. Many times it's in the discussions and seeing it from another perspective that cause things to really be driven in for us. I hope you will take advantage of that and use this as a resource to help you think about your journey.

Just FYI—the last time I was at Disney World we rode Space Mountain four times! Every time was a lot of fun, but while the ride is really cool, what's even cooler to me is that every time I ride Space Mountain I remember being a little boy riding it with my Dad. When I was a kid on Space Mountain, I was super-scared. But I knew that my Dad was with me. That roller coaster has become a God-picture for me. And the same principle that I find in it holds true for you—no matter where you are as you're holding this book, your heavenly Father is with you. How cool is that?

So sit back and get ready…It's going to be quite a ride!

HALT! DISMOUNT AND BE RECOGNIZED.

WHAT'S UP WITH THE TITLE?

In the fall of 1996 I was just a young pup in college and was asked to speak at a retreat for the church I grew up in. It was a student retreat for middle and high school students. I remember being really excited about the opportunity—it was my first "real" opportunity as an adult to go speak to students. I was a tad bit nervous! (It didn't help that I got really lost on the way there, but that's another story.)

This was the trip that I really connected with a student who would eventually become almost like my little brother. His name is Derek and now he is some famous guitar player for a rock band. Back then he was just a goofy 6th grader who liked sports and rock-and-roll guitar. It would be an understatement to say that we connected pretty quickly.

One afternoon during the retreat I was taking a walk around this really cool property and I saw *it!* From the corner of my eye I saw something that looked like a really old sign sticking up out of the ground. I went over to it and pulled it out. It was pretty nasty and dirty, so I cleaned it off. On one side it said "Come Again Soon" and on the other side it said, "Halt! Dismount and Be Recognized." I thought it looked pretty cool so I kept it.

I found out later that the place we were staying used to be a resort for people back in the day when they came in on horse and carriage.

The sign was at the gate for a long time to let riders know to stop, get off the horse, and let the staff know that they had arrived.

For over 10 years this sign (which by the way is the cover of the book) has been with me. It was in my dorm room in college and has followed me to wherever I have lived. It's one of the first things I have to find a strategic place for when I move somewhere new.

As I started writing this book I was thinking about a title—I went through a ton of titles. Some of the titles I came up with I thought were pretty cool, but honestly most were pretty stupid and cheesy. I still think that "Fully Exposed" is a cool title, but for some reason many thought it could be a little shady. One of my friends wants me to take a picture on a bearskin rug and make that the cover. Yeah—try to get that visual out of your mind!

Around November of 2006 I was really struggling with what they call "writer's block." (Whoever "they" are.) I started praying and asking God for some more clarity and direction. As odd as it sounds one night while thinking about this, I just stared at this sign for a long time. It was so obvious—not only has this sign been with me for a long time, but it also perfectly helps describe the message of what this book is about.

So that's how the book got its title. As I write this I'm staring at the sign thinking of all the life that has been lived while having that thing around. I think about this crazy journey that God has us all on called life. I think of how amazing it is that He actually cares about each of our journeys individually.

As you jump into this book my hope is that you will be able to reflect a bit on your own journey and what God is doing in and through your life. I can't wait to share some of my journey with you! (That means you need to keep reading!)

HALT!

"Halt" isn't a word you hear everyday in America. In England that's another issue, but in America "halt" isn't a frequently used word. We tend to use the word "stop."

What does it mean to you to stop? Does it mean to simply slow down or is there another meaning? Could it be to cause something to quit doing something else—like I am going to "stop" playing video games now because I need to do homework? I need to "stop" and get off Facebook because I'm going to see my friends soon at school anyway? (Many of the guys in my small group check Facebook before they go to school everyday and as soon as they get home which makes me wonder, *why do you check it right before you're about to see everyone*? That's what I get for wondering!)

Think about it for a second: What does it mean to you to stop?

I know for me, being told to stop typically means to quit something that I'm enjoying doing. Most of the time in my life when I've been told to stop it causes some tension. To be honest usually I don't want to be told to stop. (Unless, of course, you're in a fast car with blue lights and a siren, and then I'm happy to stop.)

How about you? Do you like stopping? When you think about the word, what kind of feeling does it brew up in your heart?

Think about when you were younger and your parents to told you to stop something. How did you feel? I always hated it when my parents would tell me to stop watching TV and go to bed since I had to go to school. I don't like it when I'm working on something and have to stop to do something I don't want to do. Why is that?

I think in all of us there is a sense of struggle when we're told what to do. That sense can really cause some weird feelings and actions. But I'm learning that we need to find a way to fight that sense and stop. Why?

In the first part of this book we're going to hit the brakes for a bit and think about halting. I am learning that it's critical to our lives to be able to find some time and stop. Even if the thought of coming to a halt drives you crazy, you're already doing it aren't you? You're stopping long enough to read this! It's time to hit the brakes and think about stopping for a moment. Stopping in the present could actually be the best decision that you could make for your future…

Read on and you'll find out why!

A Lot of Noise

I have a TON of noise in my life. And by noise I don't just mean loud sounds. (But I do like my music loud!) Noise is not only sounds; it's also events and things that can cause distraction in our lives, minds, and hearts. I recently asked some students about some of the noises in their lives—here are some of the things they came up with:

"Noises in our lives"

* Cell phones
* Text messaging
* Instant messaging
* MySpace/Facebook
* Email
* Music
* TV
* Movies
* The Internet
* Video games
* Friends
* What others wear
* Gossip
* Talking
* Listening
* The radio
* Pets
* Relationships
* Teachers
* Homework
* Practice
* Work
* Working out
* Food
* Decisions
* Thinking

* Driving
* Parents
* Peer pressure
* Cars
* Church
* Brothers/sisters
* Loneliness
* Growing up

And that's the short list! Think about it—we all have a lot of noise in our everyday life. I'm the king of noise. I love it. I'm what you call a serious multi-tasker. If you could follow me for a day I might just drive you crazy. It has happened to others! I always have some type of music playing. It's not unusual for me to be at my office with music going, while I'm reading an email, typing another email, text messaging, reading a document, writing a document, drinking coffee, and thinking about lunch. Yep. Welcome to my world.

I love noise! I started thinking about it and even on my drive into work it's usually pretty noisy. I have the radio or my trusty iPod rolling, I'm thinking about my day, usually texting someone, thinking about whether or not to stop at Starbucks (yet), and oh yeah—driving!

It's so easy for all this noise in our lives to simply drown out other noise. Here's the scary thing: Because of all this noise, many of us couldn't hear God if we wanted to because we've put way too much stuff between Him and us. God speaks to us through many things— His Word (The Bible), His people, and His creation are just a few. He also speaks through things like music and even books. The danger for you and I is that although God is speaking, we might not be listening. One reason for that is because of all this noise we have invited into our everyday life.

This reality is where the HALT! part of our journey is *so* incredibly important. If you and I were to find time to stop and really try and listen and look for God in and around our lives, we just might see and hear Him. To do that just might mean turning down all of our noise and focusing some of our attention on trying to really listen to God and what He is saying to our hearts and what He is doing in our lives. How much noise do you have? Are you ready to turn it down? Can you even really understand what you are reading right now because of all the other noise in your life? Turn if off. Turn it down. Take some of your energy and focus it in on trying to hear the things God is trying to say to you right now.

Once you start hearing from Him, you will discover a pattern of how God speaks to you in your life. If you are not listening ... you will not hear. It's time to start listening, my friend. In many ways the quality and direction of your life depends on it!

Be Still

I think we've landed on the truth that we all have a lot of noise in our lives. Here is the serious danger in all this noise— if our lives are so full of noise, chances are we can't hear God!

Now I'm no expert on this, but I've been learning a lot about it recently. I've discovered one of the craziest remedies to noise that you've ever heard of. Honestly, if you can find a way to apply it to your life it'll blow your mind. Want to know what it is?

Be still.

Seriously.

Stop.

Be Still.

Find a spot and practice solitude. Solitude is a big word that means to be in quiet and silence.

At least 2-3 times a week I'm trying to intentionally practice silence. Sometimes on my drive into work I'll intentionally turn my cell phone off, have no radio or iPod on, and just take some time and be quiet. I ask God to help me to just be quiet and I do my very best to listen to Him. It's tough. Usually my mind wanders off and I'm thinking about something else. But I'm learning about trying to really simply focus on God.

To help me practice solitude, I try to go somewhere and just chill for a bit. Sometimes it's my back porch. Sometimes it's taking the dog for a walk. But it always is a time of intentionally stopping from my usual busyness to try and listen to God and my heart. I've found that the more time I spend listening to God in silence and solitude, the easier it is for me to really hear Him when the day and my life gets a little noisier.

I've tried doing this with several groups of students that I've had a chance to speak to. About halfway through my talk I ask them to be still and silent for just five minutes and simply think and be open to hear from God. You should see how some people squirm just trying to be quiet and still for five minutes! (Oh wait, I'm that way too.)

When the five minutes is up you would think they haven't spoken to anyone in years. It's crazy—everyone lets out a collective breath and immediately starts talking to their friends. Why is that?

When I ask if it was hard, most students say it was. Why? Because being still and quiet is something that we just don't do very often.

Before you move onto the next section of the book, my challenge for you is this: HALT!

Find some time in your life—maybe it's right now—to simply be quiet for as long as you can. Simply be. Allow your Creator to restore your heart and love you like only He can. Allow Him total access to your heart and ask Him to do whatever He needs to do to help restore your heart so you can be the person He has put you here to be.

Let me encourage you to find some time to make halting a regular part of your life. Here's why it's so important: On the journey of your life it's incredibly important to know where you are. If you're not taking time to stop and be still, you might not have any idea what direction your life is going in.

You don't want to be that person who one day looks in the mirror and asks him or herself, "How in the world did I get here?"

I'm learning that one of the wisest things we can do in our lives is to regularly stop and take stock of where our life is. The best way to do that is to simply halt and check in with God.

Doing this has honestly how I handle my life. I can see a difference in my life when I'm not taking time to do this regularly. I can also see how it helps me when I'm regularly finding time to stop.

Oh yeah, Jesus did this too. Mark 1:35 records Jesus going to a solitary place to stop and pray. As the pastor of my church always says: "If it's good enough for Jesus, it's good enough for me."

Before you move into the book I want to ask you to really think about how you can make some time to HALT! Again, maybe that means that you need to put this book down right now and simply stop and talk to God about where your life is going. Maybe you need to go outside. Take a walk. Find a quiet place at your house. Just go. Your heart desperately needs some solitude. I hope you can find it and allow your Heavenly Father to take care of the part of you He cares the most about!

Like a Deer

Recently I was at a retreat in the northern mountains of Georgia. One night after our sessions were done, the guys and I were hanging out on the back porch. Guys, you know what I'm talking about! Ladies, let me fill you in: This is where we go to have story time. This is where we catch up by telling our funniest, grossest, or craziest stories we've accumulated since the last time we hung out.

We were just talking away when suddenly one guy says: "Did you hear that?" I didn't hear anything. Then he says: "I heard something in the woods." Of course our manly instincts kick in and we all walk over to the patio railing to see what we can spot.

And then it happened. A *big* deer walked directly in front of us. We were about 20 feet above ground on the patio. The deer walked right under us and just stopped. He looked around and even looked our way for a moment. After a few minutes he wandered off and we all sat there amazed that this creature was so close. And then we heard more noise and a bunch of deer ran in front of us. It was pretty cool.

Now, for the most part, I'm a city boy. My dad has been known to (legally) shoot a few deer here and there, but that's not my scene. (I think Saturdays in the fall are best used for eating chili and watching college football.) All that to say, I have not come in super-close contact with deer in my life.

You know what was amazing about this event? We were quiet. The guys and I were pretty loud and then we were silent when we were in the presence of the deer. Why? Because we all knew that if we were loud the deer would run away. We didn't want that, so we stayed quiet because we were excited about being in the presence of this large, magnificent creature.

Later that night I started thinking. (It happens every now and then.) Here is the thought that kept running through my mind: "Why can I shut up and be quiet for a simple deer, yet so often I don't shut up and acknowledge the presence of my heavenly Father?"

It's true. I guess if I were around deer all the time it wouldn't be a big deal if one walked right in front of me. The truth is that God is always with us so I guess it becomes just another part of life.

But, wait a minute! That's not right!

God, the Creator of the heavens and the earth wants to have a personal relationship with us. He wants to lead and guide our lives. He wants to talk to us like our friends talk to us. But for most of us, we know that and aren't truly experiencing it? Why is that?

Why can we stop for things that seem special at the time, but not for the Person who should be the most important One in our lives? That night with the deer caused me to really think about what I think about God being here. It's easy to think of God being God in heaven. It's not as easy to think that because of the Holy Spirit that God is always with us. Even more mind boggling than that, He's in us.

Maybe, just maybe, if we take the time to recognize whose presence we're in we'd be in awe of God being here right now. As you read these words the Creator of the universe is here. Right now in this place. He is with you.

How does that make you feel?

What causes you to stop?

I hope and pray that you are reminded today that the God that hung the stars is with us right now in this moment. As you hold this book, your Heavenly Father is longing to simply be with you. That's why it's important to halt! For many of us it's in the stopping that we take time to focus on hearing and knowing what's really going on around us.

So…what's going on in your world today? You have an incredible opportunity right now to put this book down, take a deep breath and listen. God is here. God is now. He wants you to know that He's here and for you to hear Him. Are you listening?

Did You Say Something?

Have you ever heard of selective listening? Of course you have. You know, that's when your mom or dad asks you to take the trash out and you act like you didn't hear what they said so you keep doing whatever else it is you're doing. When they ask you why you didn't take the trash out you say: "I didn't hear you ask me to do that."

Right.

You know you did. Here's a clue…so do they.

You just chose not to listen. You were selectively listening. Imagine if I was to walk up to you and offer you a brand-new car and have the keys in my hand. Would you listen then? Of course you would!

Why do we sometimes choose to listen and other times choose not to?

For many of us it's because we get too preoccupied with so much other stuff.

For the last few chapters we have been talking about stopping and trying to listen to God. I'm not sure what that means to you, but let's take a moment and think about how God speaks to us. This is important for you and I because it would be cool to just know that we need to stop and listen, but if we don't know what we are listening for and how God speaks, then we are missing out!

Here are a couple of ways that I've have seen or heard God speaking to me in my everyday life. Please don't hear me say that I'm an expert on this. I get so distracted and have selective listening to God way too often. But, my hope is that by us talking about this is that we will have our radars up and aware of what God is trying to say to us today. So think about this…

God speaks through many things.

This is an interesting part of God's character. In modern day Christianity, God doesn't necessarily speak in an audible voice. He speaks through His Word (the Bible) He speaks through His Spirit in us (the Holy Spirit) He speaks through nature, He speaks through music, He speaks through life experience, He speaks through others, and He even speaks through silence. He seems to use different things to speak to every person in their own way. You and I could read the same Bible verse and hear two different things. We could sit at the beach and hear different things from God. We could hear a great song and God could use it to speak to us in different ways. He speaks to us through prayer. He speaks to us through history. He speaks to us through our gifts and talents. He speaks to us through love. He speaks to us through relationships. He speaks to us through culture. The bottom line is that God speaks through many things! Our part is that we need to be listening.

God's words always come with a feeling of peace and warmth.

No matter how old I am, there is something comforting about my dad's voice. Just yesterday I called him to help me figure out how to fix something at my house. You see, he knows how to do that stuff because he has been there and done that. He didn't freak out or get upset; he simply told me what I needed to do. Just letting him know the problem and searching for a solution made me feel better. Do you get the connection? It's the same way with our Heavenly Father. When we take the issues and concerns of our life to Him and listen to Him, there will be at some point a sense of peace and even warmth that comes from that. I'm not saying it's going to immediately be better and things are going to work out the way you want it to. In fact, that rarely happens. But when you run to your Heavenly Father you allow Him to give you the love, encouragement, and direction that you can only get from Him.

God's words always line up with the Bible.

This might sound simple, but it's important. We get mixed messages from our world. It's important when we're listening to God to do our best to search the Bible to see how what we're hearing lines up to His Word. This can be a tough one for us. It's tough because none of us can fully understand God! I would encourage you as you're listening to God to find someone you trust that is further down the road in his or her journey with God. As you wrestle with listening to God and lining it up to His word, ask that person (or people) to help you dig in and discern what God might be saying to you. This is another reason why it's great to study and read the Bible, it really does help us hear and understand God more and more.

God is always speaking to us. I am learning that one of the best things we can do in our lives is to learn how to halt and listen to what God is trying to say to us. I will say it again; I think many times we can't hear God speaking to us because of all the stuff we have in our lives. It's time to turn that noise down and turn our hearts and ears toward God.

Oh yeah, and think about this. What happens if your mom or dad asked you to take out the trash and you did it right then? You know what happens: you have a feeling of accomplishment that all is well in your world. You know that you are doing your best to listen and follow those who have been given leadership in your life. In the same way, it would be really wise for you and I to start doing a better job of listening and responding to God's voice in our lives.

And that starts with halting.

Making It Personal

Something really cool just happened to me. A few weeks ago a friend of mine called and invited me to come to a conference he was hosting. This particular conference is a big deal in conference world and he told me that he had a few guys he wanted me to meet with to talk about this book. I was excited about the opportunity to talk about what you're now holding in your hands.

So I left work and headed over the to conference center to make my meeting. I get a little bit of a run around and at one point I was told to sit in the front row of the arena and wait. The guy wasn't able to meet with me at the time we were supposed to, and they asked if I could wait until the next session was over. Luckily I didn't have anything else to do for a few hours and thought it would be cool to catch a session anyway. So I stayed and just chilled in the front row where they asked me to sit. A few friends came by and it was cool to catch up with some folks. All the while I was wondering about the runaround I was getting.

So the program started. The guy who called me (Reggie) was actually one of the emcees for the event. Reggie was up front and doing his thing and then he asked a question: "How many of you have been small group leaders before? Please stand up." I, along with an arena full of people, stood up.

Reggie then said that he wanted to have some students tell some stories about their small group leader. He brought six students up front. As they walked by to take the stage something was obvious… and it was cool. I'll share about that in a moment.

One by one Reggie interviewed these 6 guys who range from age 15 to age 25. Each shared a story about how their small group leader had been there for them during a moment in their life. They shared about a late night call. They shared about tough decisions their small group leader helped them through. They shared about some defining moments in their faith that their small group leader walked through with them. It was amazing. It was powerful. All I could do was stare and be proud.

After they all shared Reggie said, "These guys have a common bond, they have all had the same small group leader." That bond…

was me. Reggie brought me to his conference (called the Orange Conference) to give me "The Orange Award." He asked me to come up and they gave me an award. It was a powerful moment and one I will not soon forget.

This just happened a few days ago, but I'm still in awe of that moment. God used that moment to give me just a small glimpse of encouragement about the relationships He has called me to build in my life.

I'm not writing this to boast about an award I got for simply doing what I love to do. I'm writing this to share with you another important part of the HALT process. That part is the relational part.

We can bring your life a halt.

We can listen and make sure your heart is in the right place.

If we do both of these and have no relationship with the One we're trying to listen to, then we're missing something aren't we?

To have a relationship with someone means that you have a connection with that person. Some relationships are incredibly personal while some are very impersonal.

I have an impersonal relationship with the President. I've heard him speak a lot. I know many of the things that he says and does. But I don't know him. I can't call him up right now and invite him to come over for dinner tomorrow night. Chances are I can't zip him a text and see if he wants to grab some coffee. (Although that would be pretty cool.) I have an impersonal relationship with him.

Many of us are great at having impersonal relationships. We have them with celebrities, athletes, and even at times famous people in our own community. We can sit around and talk about them all the time, but the reality is we really don't know them. In fact, some of us have impersonal relationships with the very people we live with! (Ouch!)

Imagine if your whole life was built around impersonal relationships— a bunch of people you knew about, but really didn't know. That would really stink wouldn't it?

Think about this— we all have a group of people in our lives that we have personal relationships with. It could be your family, friends, teammates, co-workers or even your pet. You have a connected relationship with plenty of people. These are the most important relationships in your life. These are the people who will be there for you. There are the people you're doing life with.

In the beginning of this chapter I shared with you about the award I got a few days ago. Can I share with you the coolest part of that day? It wasn't getting applause from almost 4,000 people. It wasn't the surprise of getting the award. It wasn't even that so many of my friends were there to experience that moment with me.

The best part of getting that award was hearing each of the 6 guys share their story of our relationship and how God has used it. That's some seriously powerful stuff, my friend. I didn't cry that day. I'm not sure why I didn't; I think I was so overwhelmed that I couldn't. I did that night though. You know why? Real relationships are emotional. Real relationships have great value. There is something incredibly powerful when you really get to dig in and have a real relationship with someone.

So in the last few chapters you've thought about halting and trying to listen to God. A huge part of being able to listen to Him is to have a personal relationship with Him. Think about these verses for a moment:

"This is how much God loved the world: He gave his Son, his one and only Son. And this is why: so that no one need be destroyed; by believing in him, anyone can have a whole and lasting life. God didn't go to all the trouble of sending his Son merely to point an accusing finger, telling the world how bad it was. He came to help, to put the world right again. Anyone who trusts in him is acquitted; anyone who refuses to trust him has long since been under the death sentence without knowing it. And why? Because of that person's failure to believe in the one-of-a-kind Son of God when introduced to him." (John 3:16-18 MESSAGE).

Our heavenly Father wants to have a PERSONAL relationship with you. He has done what it takes to re-connect you to Him. God wants to have a really close relationship with you. He doesn't desire to have an impersonal relationship with you. He doesn't desire to have a semi-personal relationship with you. In fact, He helps make it right for us to experience relationship the way it was intended to be experienced.

I don't know about you, but when I hear this it might seem a bit unbelievable. Honestly, if *You* created the stars and sustain the galaxies: *why do You care about me?* Here is why it's so important that we have a personal relationship with God. If not, then He is just some cosmic being that seems cold and impersonal. Luckily the Bible tells us that He cares about us individually. He wants to talk to us. He wants to hear about our thoughts, struggles, feelings and triumphs. You are as important to God as any person on this planet. Why? That's because **He created you to know HIM personally.**

If you're going to HALT and think about where your life is, can I suggest a big first step? Think about your personal relationship with God. How personal is it right now? (Scary thought: He already knows everything about our lives. Life altering thought: He still loves us anyway!)

As you think about what you're reading, I hope you can make it personal between you and our God. Much like that day at the conference, you'll quickly discover how powerful, emotional, and meaningful a real relationship can be.

Dig Deeper

Here are some things you can use to help make what you just read more personal.

Here are some songs that will help you connect to this part of the book. As you listen to them, think about what you just read and how it connect from your ears to your heart.

"Come and Listen" by the David Crowder* Band from the CD *A Collision*
"Stop the World" from the Matthew West CD *Something To Say*
"Adding to the Noise" from the Switchfoot CD *The Beautiful Letdown*
"You Are God" sung by Charlie Hall on the Passion CD *God of This City*
"God Is With Us" from the Michael Olson CD *Where Fear and Faith Collide*
"Right Here" from the Jeremy Camp CD *Stay*
"Help Me to Find You" from the Todd Fields CD *Free*
"Stillness (Speak to Me)" from the Aaron Shust CD *Anything Worth Saying*
"You and I" from the Future of Forestry CD *Twilight*
"Call My Name" from the Third Day CD *Revelation*

Here are some Bible verses to help you think about what you just read:

Psalm 46:10
Psalm 131:2
Zephaniah 3:17
Mark 1:35
John 10:26-28
Romans 7:15-20

Here are some questions to help you think about what you just read. You can think about these on your own, or you can find a group of friends you trust, read this together, and then talk about these questions.

- What does it mean to you to halt?
- How did the story about the deer connect with you?
- How do you connect with knowing how easily we stop for some things but usually not for God?
- Think about the deer story—what does it mean to you that God is always near you?
- Think about your own life for a minute. What are some noises that are going on in your heart and mind right now?
- What are some things that might be preventing you from being able to really listen to God?
- How do you think your life might be different if you regularly took time to stop and clear your heart and mind? What about if you knew God was always with you- how would you live?
- Why do you think most of us have a hard time actually doing that?
- Share a story about a time when you practiced "selective listening."
- How do you think that God speaks to you?
- Think about all of your relationships. Who are the people you are closest with? How would you describe those relationships?
- If you are really honest; how really personal are those relationships? (Do you feel comfortable sharing anything or only certain things?)
- Why do you think so many of us have trouble getting personal in relationships?
- How personal is your current relationship with God?
- How personal do you want your relationship with God to be? Why?

* Take a moment and write out what your weekly schedule looks like. Be honest! Include everything; sleep, TV, computer, practice, school, eating and really everything you can think that makes a typical week for you.

Now that you've written out what a typical week looks like for you, think about this: "When can I find some time to HALT during my week?" Look at your schedule; it's there! Write some time into your schedule in the coming week to stop, think, be quiet, and simply give God your heart and mind. Think about halting for a minute. Ask God to help you to turn down that noise and really hear Him.

DISMOUNT

Our next step in the journey is "Dismount." Dismount basically means to get down from or off of something. In the context of a journey, we usually don't dismount until we've stopped. You don't jump out of the car until you get where you're going, right? It takes getting somewhere and stopping before you move on. With this in mind, since we've talked about stopping, now we're going to dismount. That means taking a moment and thinking about where we are.

In my life *I am where I am because of where I've been.* Yeah, I know it's a weird sentence, but read it again. You are who you are based on where you've been. It's true!

We are all where we are as a result of events, relationships, and opportunities that we've had so far in our lifetime. One way to know where we are is to take a look back at where we've been.

In this section of the book there are a bunch of short "glimpses" of the journey from my life. These stories have been taken over the last few years of thinking and journaling as things have happened and as I've looked back. God breathes into my everyday because He promises that He's with me always. Sometimes I've been able to actually see Him in those present moments, but sometimes I've had to look backwards in order for me to see Him. I've heard it said that hindsight is 20/20—and I've found that to be true when it comes to seeing God in my life. As we walk through some of my everyday life moments in the next few chapters, hopefully you'll see how they collide with an incredible God.

I hope as you walk through this section you'll see yourself in these pages somehow, and that'll cause you to step back in your own life. In other words, I hope it helps you dismount and know where you are. Happy trails, my friend!

From the Back Porch...

Let me set the scene for you: I'm writing this on my laptop, sitting on the back patio of an amazing cabin in the Carolina mountains. (Some friends are graciously letting me use their cabin for a week while I'm working on this!) Directly in front of me are mountains literally as far as I can see. Last night as I sat out here and looked up, I've never seen so many stars just hanging brightly in the sky before in my life. It was simply unbelievable. There aren't words to describe how amazing it was. I don't know how you could look at a scene like that and wonder if there is a Creator. His design is literally written in the heavens.

Right now the sky is a clear, bright, crisp blue. Off in the distance are a few really fluffy clouds that are just dangling in the middle of all of the blue. The birds are chirping. The sun is shining and the breeze is picking up a little—it's early fall in the mountains. The leaves on the trees are moving along with the wind. Oh yeah—there are tons of trees surrounding the cabin. A squirrel just jumped trees right in front of me. I just refreshed my coffee and the music coming from my laptop is working in tandem with nature to help set the mood. (I'm currently listening to the "Mountains" playlist on my iTunes.)

So have you got the scene? Can you picture it? Can you feel it? The fresh air. The breeze. The trees. The mountains. The sky. The beauty. The golf balls?

Yep, to my left is...a golf course. The cabin is directly next to a hole on a golf course in the mountains. In front of me is a picture of nature that's perfect for a postcard and to my left is...a golf course. This is really very funny to me. Why? I've had some very bad moments of shame on the golf course. I have a problem with golf—I stink. Seriously, I'm afraid to call myself a golfer for fear that someone will hear that and then actually see me play and misrepresent the name golfer. I'm that bad. But you know what? I love the game.

I used to wonder who actually watched golf on TV. Now I do. I'm that guy. The last few years I've fallen in love with this game. I even subscribe to the magazines now. For some really strange reason, I think I should be a good golfer. I'm not sure exactly why, but the competitive guy inside me hates the fact that I stink. Sometimes that comes out in my language, sometimes it even comes out in thrown clubs. (If you throw your club further than the ball went, can you spot the ball there?) Once I was so mad with a poor shot I'd just made that I threw my club in anger and my club landed in the bunker. Seriously, I stink. Golf is really fun—and really FRUSTRATING!

I'm not sure why I spend so much time getting frustrated with a little white ball, but I do. And I do it again. I watch golf on TV and I'm completely amazed at how incredible the pros are. A bad day for them would be better than my best day ever. That's encouraging. Yet I still go out when I can afford it and do it all over again. I knowingly put myself in a position to get frustrated. I even tell myself: "I'm just going to have fun today and not get frustrated."

That usually lasts about a hole, maybe two.

So golf is beauty and frustration all in one.

The view I have right now is kind of the same way. Nature is right in front of me, an incredible picture of God's majesty. To my left is golf—a reminder of cussing, club-throwing frustration.

When I was sitting out here this morning it just hit me—this is probably how God sees us—beauty and frustration. The Bible tells us that He made us in His image to experience a personal relationship with Him. This is the Beauty. It also tells us that due to our sin, we have since ruined the beauty. Frustration arrives on the scene. But the story doesn't stop there. Then Scripture tells us that God sent Jesus to mend the frustration that we cause Him. We can still frustrate Him now through the way we live our lives, yet we are His. And He loves us anyway.

It's incredible to me that I am both beauty and frustration to God. The fact that that tension exists and He chooses to love me—and to love us—anyway is such a testimony to His great love.

I'm captivated just sitting here in this rocking chair and looking at both things. I just heard a golfer scream—frustration in the midst of beauty—a subtle reminder about my life. Note to self, it just might be time to take those golf lessons.

A Dog's Life

Murphy—that's my dog. As I write this he's currently two years old. He's a 90-something pound golden retriever. I've wanted to have a big dog since I was a little kid and my uncle had Josh—a very cool yellow lab. Josh was just a cool dog.

Well, I finally got one! I called a lady from the newspaper, explained my situation, and she gave me a cool deal. (Situation being a poor guy in student ministry.) So I drove home with this little seven-pound, full-breed golden retriever. He curled up and laid in my lap the whole ride home. I don't use this word much—but the boy was just cute. The ride home was pretty cool.

We got home and he was so nervous. A new place. No mom, no brothers or sisters—just me. I was lucky that day; my roommates (who are in a band) had just left to go out of town for a bit so they didn't have to deal with his first few days. He was really cautious taking his first tour of the place. It was actually pretty funny watching his little legs try and navigate through the house. Well, those little legs weren't so little after a while.

It was a fun first year with him. He chewed on everything. He ate four of my roommate's contact cases. He chewed up another roommate's custom ear molds. Basically anything that was in snout range was in play. I was cutting the grass in the backyard once when I saw him chewing—on a tree! Seriously, the dog was gnawing away at a tree? The dog has more toys than he needs, and he is chewing on a tree? Thank God for the suggestion for buying him rawhide bones. But at the same time, there's just nothing like getting up in the middle of the night to go to the bathroom and stepping on a half-chewed-up bone with your bare feet—that will check your love for your dog real quick!

Murphy has very little respect for personal space. If dogs have a love language I think his is "physical touch." His whole goal in life is to get as close to you as possible and then sneak in a lick or two. I love the hairy beast though. He is my boy.

So now the Murph is huge and destructive. When it's just the two of us at my house, he's great. He just chills out wherever I am. If I'm in my office, he lays on the floor; if I'm cutting the grass, he runs around like he has no common sense. But for the most part, he's an absolutely great dog—when it's just the two of us.

But when someone new comes in—watch out. The switch has been flipped. What happens then is a transformation from laid-back dog to one of the most energetic dogs you'll ever see. Something takes him over and he just goes out of control. Good times, friend, good times! If I've learned anything from Murphy it's the importance of showing others how excited you are to see them!

Have you ever been asleep and heard something and wondered if that was in real life or your dream? One night last fall it happened to me. Something really gross happened. (If you get grossed out easily—consider yourself warned!) I was snoring away in la la land and in my dream (or so I thought) I heard something making this really weird—yet loud—hacking sound.

And then I felt something really warm on my head. That's right, my cute little puppy had thrown up on my head.

I quickly had a choice here—I could just lay there with dog puke in my hair and go back to sleep. I could throw him out the window off the 2nd floor and just forget about him since he did something wrong. I could have compassion on him and get up and clean myself off and make sure he was okay. Of course I threw him out the window. Just kidding. (PETA people calm down—I love and take great care of Murph.) I jumped out of bed and actually cleaned him up first. Why?

Because when I bought him, I took control of his care. When I signed the papers, he was mine. If I just let him sit there sick, I would be neglecting my responsibility.

Here's why I share this story with you: This situation really reminds me of my relationship with God. Because of our imperfections, we're dirty. The Bible calls God "holy" which means He's completely clean and pure. I for sure, am not clean and perfect. I am very much imperfect. I've said many things I regret. I haven't always done the right thing. As a Christian the Bible says that Jesus paid for my sins—my imperfections. When my sins were paid for, God took control over my life. (1 Corinthians 6:20)

I learned something that night from my dog's life. I was reminded of the timeless truth that God's love for endures forever. Although I am dirty and messed up, He has still chosen to enter my world. I was bought for a price and now I am connected relationally to the One who paid that price.

Often I put God in a position to decide what to do—to forget about me, to throw me away and start over, or to clean me up and take care of me. Chances are, you put Him in the same position sometimes too. But God always makes the same decision I made with Murphy. And that my friend is good news for you and I!

A Long Day in November

November 16th 1986.

This day changed my life forever and I remember it all too well. The guys on our street had set up a huge game of neighborhood football. This was a serious game—people were riding home on our school bus with permission just so they could join in. This was the kind of game where instead of us getting out of the way of oncoming cars, cars had to stop for us because so many people were playing in the street. This was some serious neighborhood football.

My mom had been really sick for a few days. When I got home from school that day I went in to check on her—she was asleep. I changed and went outside for *the* game. It got going and it was a lot of fun. About an hour later I went inside to get a quick drink. I went back to my parents' room and found my mom—she had fallen off of her bed and her face had turned blue. I called my brother inside and we called 911. Then we called my dad and my grandparents.

Thankfully, the ambulance showed up pretty quickly. I vividly remember being shuffled into my bedroom with the dogs to keep them company while they were barking up a storm with the paramedics all over the house. It just all happened so quickly.

My dad rushed home from work and before I knew it, we were at the hospital. Doctors were trying to figure out what happened. After a few hours, we found out that my mom had experienced a massive stroke. The main artery in her brain had been clogged by a major blood clot which caused it to burst. She was in a coma, and the doctors said it was likely that she wouldn't come out of it.

Let me take a quick break and tell you something—I am a mama's boy. I love my Dad dearly; he is a very good man. I hope one day I will be as faithful and caring as he has always been to our family. But…well, Mom is just the stuff. She has the biggest heart in the world. She was president of the PTA, she was a leader in our church, she was team mom on our sports teams, and she ran her own catering company. There aren't sufficient words to explain how much I love my mom. Her love and passion for our family has always been part of the fuel that has kept us going. No matter what crazy idea or thing I've had or chased after, she has always been one of my biggest encouragers.

My first question to God about the whole situation were more like accusations: "Why her, God? She's an angel and one of the most active people in our town—and You allowed her to get sick? Why God?"

A few days later, my mom came out of her coma. As I type that out I'm still in awe of the fact that it's true. It was such a blessing, such a precious second chance. When you're in a coma, your whole body shuts down. It's kind of like when the power goes off at your house—when it comes back on you have to reset everything. Mom was back—sort of. She was in an awkward vegetative state for a little while. But God had given her a second chance.

While she was recovering from her stroke, communication was tough. One of the ways that we communicated with her was by one of us holding a yellow legal pad with the letters of the alphabet on it. We would point at it and she would nod her head and spell out words. The words were "I want to go home," "What is happening?" and things like that. A memory burned into my heart was one night we took our dogs and held them up to the window in her hospital room. She was crying and I know by their reaction that somehow the dogs knew it was Mom in that room. I had never cried so hard. It was just this moment of surrender…I was so mad because I couldn't do anything to solve this problem and I didn't know who my mom was or who she'd be after this was all over.

She slowly got better. Right before Christmas 1986 she was transferred to Warm Springs Rehabilitation Facility in Warm Springs, Georgia. (It's the rehab center that FDR made famous). The people on staff there were just unbelievable. But even still, that was a weird Christmas.

That year we were "that" family that churches collected stuff for. I am pretty sure I ate enough green bean casseroles during that time to carry me for life. As I look back, I'm thankful that we lived in a smaller town where people knew each other and cared. I actually still live in that town—it's now much larger and suburban. And frankly, it seems like most people simply don't care about other people as much anymore.

Mom had to learn how to talk, walk, write, and read all over. Everything slowly came back to her. It was weird to be in school myself yet know that my mom was coloring and trying to stay in between the lines. We spent Christmas there in her room at the rehab facility.

A few months later, Mom came home. Slowly but surely she adapted back to life. It took a while for me to get used to her being back on the scene—I wanted her to be the same person she was before, but the reality was that she wasn't that person anymore. That's the reality of serious medical incidents like these—they change things.

Here is the supernaturally cool thing: If you met my mom now, you'd never know what happened. It's amazing. She gets sick easier now; her immune system isn't the best. But you know what? She's alive! God gave her more time on this planet to help do what she does—love people. Mom loves people; she loves teaching little kids about Jesus and His love for us. She loves serving at her church and being the hands and feet of Christ wherever she goes. I meet very few people in my life that are as giving as my parents—they truly are unsung heroes, they do so much for others behind the scenes. I'm very proud to be their son.

I look back now and still don't completely understand why God allowed that to happen. The financial burden of all this was quite massive to say the least. But I do honestly believe that God allowed Mom to get sick. Twenty years later, I know what happened on November 16, 1986, still marks who I am as a person and as a child of God. I learned about trying to trust God when things don't make sense. I learned that life rarely goes as we planned. I learned a lot about what it means to cling onto faith when it's all you have.

Here is a total God thing: In my last 10 years of student ministry I've encountered countless students and families who are struggling with some kind of medical situation. I always go back to how faithful God was to our family. I go back to all the questions I asked God and all the anger I had at Him. Yet He has used it—I've been able to offer hope and encouragement to so many simply because of this event that happened on one very long day in November.

One hard reality of life is this: trouble will come into your life. Someone you know will likely get sick, or go through some kind of dramatic life event. It might even be you.

And you will make it. Not because you're really strong. Not because you've "got it in you." But because God will walk you through it.

No matter what's going on in your life right now, God will walk you through it. No matter what curve balls are being thrown your way right now, your heavenly Father is more than aware of your situation. Please know that He is right there with you in the middle of your storm. What I have found to be true it this: God doesn't stand apart from our hard times. He doesn't stand detached. But He enters in, He's right there with us. He's not just watching to see how we get through it like a spectator; He's walking through it with us every step of the way.

I love the story in the Bible when Jesus is asleep on the boat. This is right after He just did a major miracle. I don't know about you, but I know when I do a major miracle, it's time for a little rest. (That was sarcasm.) So Jesus is in the boat cabin sawing some logs (in other words, totally sleeping) and a storm starts brewing. The disciples flip out. It starts seriously storming. The boat starts to toss and turn in the rough wind and waves. The waves are crashing and the disciples are getting really nervous about their situation. Then someone has the idea: "Hey, let's go get Jesus up and let Him know it's raining."

Can you imagine what Jesus was thinking? Here He has just performed a major miracle—feeding 5,000 people with the Biblical equivalent of a Happy Meal—and His main followers were freaking out over some rain and wind. And these are the guys He was handing the faith over to!?! No wonder He needed a nap. Seriously though—the disciples were in the boat with Jesus. Miracle-working-Son-of-God Jesus. He knows all. He is in charge of it all. Yet they thought it would be smart to alert Him—the Creator of weather—of the weather crisis. I'm not implying that the disciples were numskulls with little faith, I'm just standing on the truth that even those closest to Jesus had a tough time completely trusting Him in the midst of the storms of life.

Jesus not only woke up and calmed the storm, He taught a great lesson. He said, *"You of little faith, why are you so afraid?" (Matthew 8:26).*

So—what are you afraid of right now?

Jesus knows what's going on in your life right now, my friend. He is in control whether you know it or not! And He will walk you through every single step—just turn your heart to Him. And not only will He walk you through your tough spot, He will somehow use this experience for good. I think back to November 16th, 1986, and I'm thankful that God choose to take our family through what He did.

That day in November changed my life—forever. For good.

Remodel
(Fall 2007)

What comes to mind when you hear the words "Home Depot?" Is it orange? Maybe it's a ginormous warehouse full of stuff?

I've made some stops into Home Depot over the years, but I don't think that I completely understood why people flock to Home Depot in droves until recently. Here's why: I just bought my first house.

Over the years I've stayed at various places and rented, but I've never owned a house. Now I do, and it's a whole new world.

That's when Home Depot enters into the picture. Now it's just not a place with thousands of light bulbs, it's a weekend warrior's paradise. It's a place where homeowners go to drool. When I was in high school I used to go to car dealerships and just look and dream, now I just go to Home Depot. "Oh look, that's a nice looking fixture."

I recently had a 15-minute conversation with someone at a Christmas party about light fixtures. Seriously? I used to make fun of those people, now I *am* one of those people. By "those people" I mean the people who go to a home improvement warehouse, spend money, and then go home and work!

Another interesting thing about my new house: It's the one I grew up in. My parents lived here for well over 35 years and recently moved somewhere else. They sold me the house and now I'm in the middle of remodeling it to be a little more my style and taste, whatever that is.

So I'm at full remodel stage right now. Most of my free time and money is being spent toward moving this place to being my home. As I write this I'm actually living in the basement since the upstairs is a bit of a mess—there's no carpet on the floors and I'm in the middle of changing out every light, fan, and painting in just about every room.

What's crazy is I actually lived in the basement in high school and for a spell when I first came home from college to work with a high school ministry.

So with so many memories with this house you're probably wondering, "Why are you remodeling your house?" (Well, you might not have been thinking that, but you are now!)

It's strange, but I don't want to live in my parents' house. I love my parents and liked the house when they lived here, but now they don't and I do. It's my season to make this place my own, so it's okay if I make changes that fit me.

I was a little nervous when I told my parents I was going to make some dramatic changes to the house. I wasn't sure what they were going to say. But I shouldn't have worried. They said, "Do whatever you want, it's your place now."

Here's my point in all of this: God has given you things to manage. It might be friendships, relationships, money, and even leadership. What you do with those is your choice—it's *yours*. But, the best thing we can do is to realize that it has been given to us for a reason and it's our challenge to be a good steward of it. God has given us the opportunities we're faced with, the possessions we have, and He asks us to manage them well. He's given us responsibility with freedom, and we can make it ours while honoring Him.

I don't know about you, but at times I am not that great at managing things. I have definitely dropped the ball a time or two! Have you ever walked into class and the teacher asked you to turn in the paper you completely forgot about? Ever forget about a meeting you were supposed to be at? Have you ever told someone you would do something and forget about it?

Welcome to the real world. It's tough work dealing with responsibility!

I heard something a long time ago that was tattooed on my heart. "You have the least amount of responsibility today than you will ever have the rest of your life" The speaker was talking about the truth that as we grow older and experience more things, more is expected of us. As we gain wisdom and knowledge, we are actually expected to do something with it!

In the book of Luke in the Bible there is an account of a conversation between Jesus and one of his closest followers, Peter. Jesus tells Luke a story with a point. The point of the story is "*From everyone who has been given much, much will be demanded; and from the one who has been entrusted with much, much more will be asked." (Luke 12:48)* You might have heard this before: "To whom much is given, much is expected."

That's called responsibility. Many of us are not very good about handling it. In fact, there are many of us who are not given of it because we are bad managers of the things we've been given. I'm not sure where this chapter finds you, but I know that either now or in the future you will have to handle something important.

I believe that God gives us many of these opportunities for responsibility to help us understand Him. You see, God is in the remodeling business too. When you begin a relationship with Him the Bible calls you a "new creation." (*2 Corinthians 5:17*) That does not mean that you wake up the next day and all of a sudden know the whole Bible. That doesn't mean that you won't deal with struggles anymore. This verse is talking about the truth that God is constantly molding and working in our hearts. He is constantly remodeling us to help us fully experience Him.

I've learned that remodeling is tough work. It's not easy to peel back the layers of old stuff that's built up over time. So the house is slowly coming along. And with every nail hammered in and every brush of a paintbrush I am reminded that not only am I remodeling this house, but God is always in the process of remodeling me. And that is a very good thing!

DIG DEEPER — PART I

Here are some songs that will help you connect a little more with what you just read. As you listen to them, think about what you just read and how it connect from your ears to your heart.

"Cry Out to Jesus" from the Third Day CD *Wherever You Are*
"My Hope" from The David Crowder Band CD *Can You Hear Us?*
"You Are My Hope" from the Skillet CD *Alien Youth*
"Faithful" from the Fee CD *We Shine*
"You Never Let Go" from the Passion CD *Everything Glorious*
"Beautiful" from the Shawn McDonald CD *Simply Nothing*
"A Beautiful Collision" from The David Crowder Band CD *A Collision*
"Only Hope" from the Switchfoot CD *New Way to Be Human*

Here are some verses to check out based on what you read:

Isaiah 64:8
Psalm 18:19
Psalm 130:5
Matthew 8:26
Romans 8:28
1 Corinthians 6:18-20

Here are some questions to help you think about what you just read:

- What was your favorite chapter from this section? Why?
- What is something you connected with in this section?
- What are some things you've done that might have caused you to wonder if God still loved you?
- "From the Back Porch" shared that we are often beautiful and frustrating to God at the same time. How do you relate to that?

- In "A Long Day in November" I shared about my mom getting sick and the natural questions about God that came from that. Share a time when something happened that caused you to question God.
- Did that cause you to push away or draw closer to God? Why?
- Why do you think that moments like these have such an affect on our faith?
- What is something you want to apply to your life this week based on what you read in this section?

In "A Dog's Life," I shared about my dog Murphy getting sick and three options of things he could do. Because of the commitment I made to care for Murphy, I chose to clean up the mess Murphy had made. In the same way, God has made a commitment to you.

Take a moment and think about the times He has come to your rescue to meet you right where you were. Look back on your life and see God's faithfulness. As you remember God's goodness in your life, do yourself a favor and write it down somewhere that you will remember it. There will be a season in your life when you will need to be reminded of how much God cares for you! When that season comes it will be wise to remind yourself of God's faithfulness because He will never let you go! There are times when I look at the Murph and I am reminded of that night and the commitment I've made to take care of him. In the same way if you have a relationship with Him, God has a commitment and plan for you!

That Night in Alabama...

My first semester of college, I did something that in hindsight was pretty stupid. (Okay, I did plenty of stupid things in college, but let's just leave that alone and move on.) I joined a fraternity. I'm not sure why I did it, but I did. On the front end, I loved it. I did make it through pledgeship and officially joined the fraternity as a brother. The next semester I went inactive and left the fraternity for many reasons, which I won't discuss here. But something happened during my time pledging that left a pretty interesting impression on me.

One weekend we went on a "pledge retreat" to a park in Alabama. We had to cut ourselves a walking stick and I was excited about the one I made. We got there and started setting up, and the brothers sent us in the woods to get firewood. We were told not to talk to each other, to go alone, to go pretty far away from the campsite, and to come back with a big armful of wood. So I left to go on my way.

Now, I am by nature a wanderer. I like to just go new places and wander around and get comfortable in my environment. So here I am, a freshman in college at one of the largest state parks in the country with a bunch of people I'm just getting to know, wandering around in the woods all by myself with nothing but a walking stick. Yeah. This, friend, is a recipe for something really stupid to happen. And it did.

I got lost.

Not lost like I-could-scream-and-find-my-way-back lost, I mean lost like I-am-yelling-and-hearing-nothing lost. Even though I'm a city boy, I just knew I wasn't going to die in Alabama that night. So I just calmly wandered around trying to find my way back to the group. I wandered around for over an hour. I kept looking for a road because I figured if I found a road, I could follow it back to the main road, and then get to our campsite.

Finally after a lot of wondering around I think I see a road, and I start heading that way. But I made a tragic mistake—I didn't look where I was walking.

I walked about five feet toward the road and tripped and fell... down a 30-foot-steep hill. I rolled down it, actually. Quickly. I was wearing shorts and a t-shirt, and the hill was covered in some very prickly bushes and plants. By the time I landed at the bottom of the hill I was bleeding pretty badly. I even got hit in the head with my walking stick somehow. It was one of those falls that likely wasn't even funny to watch because you knew it had to hurt. And it did.

I got up and evaluated my condition. I had wandered off the path. I had gone so far away I didn't even have an idea where home was. And all I had with me was a now-bloody stick. I stopped and prayed for a minute and just thought. I finally remembered that I thought I saw road. I climbed up the hill on the other side and right there was a road. I followed that for about 20 minutes and finally found our campsite.

I can't imagine what I looked like. I was all nasty, bloody, and beaten up. They had been looking for me, and I had been gone for over four hours.

This story is so much like so many of us. We wander off the path. We wander off into the unknown and get so far from what we know that we can't even find our way back. Just know this: No matter how far away we've wandered from God, God will always take us back.

For a lot of us, we wander so far off where we know we're supposed to be that we're just flat scared to go home again. In Luke 15, Jesus told a story, a parable, about a prodigal son. In that story, a son demands his inheritance from his father, even though his father is still alive. Cash in hand, the son leaves his father's home and goes and blows all of the money on partying and prostitution. The son's life gets so bad and he gets so desperate that he ends up taking care of pigs and is tempted to eat the garbage slop that he feeds them. After hitting rock bottom, the son goes back home in hopes that his father will take him back, not as a son, but as a hired servant. But, the father, once he sees his son coming home, joyfully sprints down the path to meet his son who has finally come home. And instead of condemning his son, he throws a huge party in his honor.

Jesus told that parable to tell about God. God is like the father in that parable, and we are like the wayward son. But when we come home to Him, He comes running. He celebrates, He rejoices, and

He's delighted. No matter what we've done, God will always take us back.

That's not a license for you to just go buck-wild whenever you want to because you know God will always clean you up. In fact, it's just the opposite. It's a call to stick with the One who will guide your life in the perfect direction for you to experience His perfect plan for your life.

If we're lost from God it's because we moved away from Him. He never moves away from us. Sometimes going back is embarrassing and even humbling, but there is something very right about being where we belong, in the arms of the One who made us. The question is: Are we ready to humble ourselves and admit that we really do need Him to help guide us? That night in Alabama I learned a lot about finding my way and always knowing that hope will carry you—even at a park in Alabama.

Supergroup

I've had the opportunity to lead small groups of students for over 11 years now. There have been times when I was leading four or five groups a week. These groups have met before school, after school, at night, and all over the place. There was definitely a season when I didn't know whether I was coming or going. If nothing else I definitely developed quite an affection for coffee!

There have been some really great groups. There have been some really tough groups. Leading each group of guys has been a great honor for me. I still think it's cool that a bunch of busy teenage guys would want to hang out and talk about God with each other. In many cases that meant getting up early and meeting for breakfast. Teenage guys getting up early...because they want to?!? That's crazy! It's cool to be a part of that.

For the last four years, God has put 12 really special and unique guys in my life. Each of them are pretty different from each other, yet possess a great heart for life and most importantly for God. They started as two different groups and then for the last year we united into one "Supergroup."

Here are some thoughts about why the "Supergroup" has been so special:

For the last four years a week doesn't go by when one of these guys will call and want to sit down and talk about something going on in his life. I haven't made a big deal out of the things going on in our large group time, in many cases the other guys didn't need to know what one of the guys was going through. In some cases, they did and it has been great watching them come around each other and do what we should do as brothers in Christ—forgive, love, and challenge each other to pursue our heavenly Father.

Almost every week I close our group with the same prayer— "God help us to be the men You have put us here to be." What has been really cool for me is watching these guys step from adolescence into manhood and more importantly step into becoming spiritual leaders.

Probably the best thing that I've ever done as a leader was to break them into smaller groups for accountability. Each week when we start they have 20-25 minutes with their partner to catch up and pray about their life and week. It's pretty tough for me to track well with 12 guys; but they can do so with each other. I've been blown away by how God has really used this to build trust, accountability, and friendships.

I've tried to be pretty intentional having time outside of our group to hang out. I love football season because every Saturday I'll make a pot of chili and anyone who wants to can come over and chill. We've had many, many game nights of cards or whatever. As much fun as these have been, the important thing for me was just having hang time outside of group to invest more in the relationships. I've learned that when it comes time for tough conversations if you don't have much invested in the relationship, you're not going to get too far. In other words, the stronger the bridge of a relationship, the more truth it can hold.

I've been really transparent with the guys and they've returned the favor. This group has been with me during some crazy times in my life, and I've chosen—for the most part—to be open about my personal struggles, whether it's in my faith, my finances, or whatever. I don't use the guys as my counselors—you have to have a line there. But I firmly believe that they need to know that following God is sometimes really tough and doesn't always make sense…yet God is still there. I hope that sharing my struggles will help build that truth into their lives.

All of them don't have a lot in common. Some guys are geared more towards sports, some towards artistic things, and some towards…well, just chilling. And that's cool. I think they've crossed the typical student barriers and chosen to trust and believe in each other. Of course there has been lots of joking and sarcasm along the way…but it has been pretty awesome to sit back and watch them interact over the last few years. Two years ago, I would've never guessed that God would've brought them to the point they're at in their relationships with each other now. What can happen when you're united by your faith is really, really cool.

More than anything else, the coolest part of this group for me has been watching many of them move from spiritual babies to some hulking men of the faith. A few years ago several of the guys weren't even walking with God. Now they're reaching out to their world and growing in their relationship with God. Their families, friends, teams, and world are different because they made a choice to be the man God has called them to be. Words can't even express how proud I am of the steps these guys have taken. They're the future leaders of college campuses, the church, and culture. I honestly believe the world will be different because these guys are living in it.

I might not have a lot to show for my life from the material standpoint. And sometimes that's a great struggle for me. It would be cool to just go buy a new SUV or a house and not have to deal with the struggles of being financially challenged. But this is something I've learned to be true—you can't put a price on eternity and the opportunity to invest in it. Knowing that, these guys make me feel like the richest man in the world. "I love you guys!" is what I tell them all the time, and I hope they can look back on their lives and feel the satisfaction I feel from being able to be a very small part of their journey. Being a part of theirs has made mine so much more fun, challenging, exciting, tough, and pretty much anything you can imagine. And I wouldn't trade it for the world.

So (finally) here is your public shout-out, guys! To Brandon, Brian, Cameron, Cody, Connor, Greg, Hans, Jared, Joe, PJ, Ryan, and Todd—thank you for allowing me to be a part of your lives. You have truly changed mine. Now it's time for you to go be the men that God has put you here to be.

We need each other. God made us that way. We need close relationships that give us room to be real. Life can be dangerous without relationships like these. This group of guys taught me how life changing it can be to trust others. This group of guys taught me about the value of being different. This group of guys taught me a lot about how a big fire can start from just a spark. The legacy of their lives will burn bright for a long, long time. And I am beyond honored to call them friends.

So…who are you doing life with?

Maybe it's time to really open up and take that step to trust someone else. I want to encourage you that if you are not currently in a group of friends talking about your faith and life…find that. It could be one of the most important decisions you ever make!

Ladies and Gentleman...an Idiot.

I've been given some really cool opportunities to communicate to students about God's love and forgiveness over the years. There are many memorable events—some which are memorable for the wrong reason. Here are just a few of my not-so-greatest hits so far:

I've spoken in front of students with the zipper in my pants down multiple times... Let's just say that can be embarrassing. I forgot to leave my cell phone in my car once—or put it on silent—and wouldn't you know the dang thing went off right at the critical end of the talk and totally ruined the moment! I've had fire alarms go off at schools—once the whole auditorium evacuated in like a minute and I was still on stage. That was awkward.

Once I left the stage at a conference and forgot to turn my microphone off. I had to go to the bathroom so bad I that I left the stage and made a quick gallop to the bathroom. I think I was praying aloud on my way down the stairs from the stage. When I was done the sound guy muted me in the conference hall, but got an earfull of what happens when I drink too much coffee in one day. That's just embarrassing right there—I'll never forget his face when I handed the microphone back to him.

I once told an FCA group that they should go around encouraging each other, that each day was "game day" and that they should be actively encouraging each other by giving each other high fives. That day every student who was there walked around school patting each other on the butt yelling: "It's game day!" Or, "Good game, man!" I got a call from the school sponsor on that one.

I almost fell asleep once on stage waiting for my turn—the music was just about to put me to sleep alongside a seriously monotone emcee. I had had a really late night and a crazy day and the combination of the two was making me doze off. When I heard, "Ladies and gentleman, our speaker tonight is..." I moved pretty quickly. I almost wanted to say "I'm sorry—let me wipe my eye crusty off real quick." But I was afraid I would wake up the students.

I was actually introduced on the spot in Romania at a student outreach as the funniest man in America. He then handed me the microphone and asked me to say something funny—there is nothing you can say at that moment that is funny after an introduction like that.

One time I spoke at a church where no one spoke English but the guy who called and asked me to come speak. Everyone else spoke Korean—and I totally didn't know that until I got there. I'm just a good 'ol boy from Georgia, and you can imagine how that went down. (Although it was pretty cool seeing my name printed in another language.) I had lots of funny stares that day.

Two friends and I once went down a flight of stairs on a sleeping bag with pots on our heads acting out a skit like we were the Jamaican bobsled team. The students at the retreat didn't laugh because we landed so hard that they thought we were hurt—and you can chalk that one up to them thinking right. I was bruised for a few weeks from that experience. We got up and they were just staring at us. They were in utter disbelief that we just took a serious tumble down a flight of stairs all for the sake of comedy. Good times.

I have many moments of forgetfulness—my favorite was when I very proudly said the wrong name of the group I was speaking to and having a student say really loudly, "Our church's name is _____." *Thanks, I think I'll just step off the stage and chew on my foot for a little while.* There have been some really bad introductions—but my all time favorite is: "Our speaker tonight is Jason Carr. He raises money for his ministry for a living. Jason, the mic's all yours." *Hmmm. Thanks for the set up pitch there, captain.*

All that to say it's quite the adventure to represent Christ. Sometimes when we attend a retreat or event, and we hear the communicator, we tend to think they have it all together. But that's so not the case. In fact there have been many times when I think I was the one in the room with the most issues to deal with! I wish I could say that I haven't been driving to speak somewhere and gotten caught up in a little road rage. (Note that I said I wish!) There have been many times when I simply didn't want to get up to talk on a specific topic because of how I'd botched it up in my own life or because of something personal I was dealing with. I remember driving to speak somewhere about relationships the day after I broke up with my girlfriend. That was tough! Recently I was having coffee with several friends who speak to students and we all were sharing some of our struggles. I wonder what the people who hear us communicate would think about all of our failures. I share this because I'm a flesh-and-blood human being who constantly makes stupid mistakes and am far from perfect. I don't expect others to be perfect because I'm fully aware that I am nowhere close to that. How about you?

We don't always know what's going on in the life of someone up front do we? I sometimes really struggle with trying to be uplifting and fun with others because I'm hurting on the inside. To be honest, some of my "best" talks have been in situations when I'm really weak and have nothing but to trust God to speak through me. There is something in knowing that you can't do something, but He can. He shows up and oftentimes shows off His glory.

I've had the chance to work with some really cool communicators over the years. They're all different in their style. One of my personal favorites was this guy who just came to serve—even though his name was on the brochure—it was about the students at the camp. He sang with the group. He ate with the group. He was not a diva—he came to serve and engage with students, and it was powerful. When he spoke they listened—why? Because they knew that he cared for them. There are some important lessons there.

One of my favorite moments ever communicating was being with some students the Monday night after 9/11. We talked about what kind of God would allow something like that to happen. Powerful stuff. Students were so open, and so was I. It was cool to see how God could take the evil intentions of a radical group and use it to draw people to Himself. I will always remember the drive home that night. I was just in awe of how amazing God really is. He seems to take our doubts and frustration and turn them into miracles.

All this to say, the next time you're listening to a communicator, take it from a not-so-good seasoned speaker—have a little grace. You have no idea what might be going on in their lives. Hopefully they're allowing God to use them and speak through them as they represent Him to you. For the teachers, coaches, youth leaders, and speakers in your life—try and drop your expectations of what or who you want them to be, and allow them to be themselves.

Oh yeah—and if you see him going onstage and you notice that his zipper is down, please tell him. He'll appreciate it. He'll be embarrassed as all get-out, but he'll appreciate it.

PK

I remember it like it was yesterday. I was downstairs away from my phone having a conversation with someone and I heard it ring and it seemed to just keep ringing. Obviously someone was trying to get in touch with me. I ran up to my phone and had a bunch of missed calls and a bunch of text messages waiting for me. In the world of student ministry, this isn't a good thing.

I remember hearing my friend tell me on the other side of the line: "Parker was just killed in a car wreck." My heart dropped down as far as it has in a long, long time.

Parker Jackson was a great kid. Like many, his life ended way too early. Parker was only 16 when he was in a car accident on November 6, 2006, and died. The affect of his life and death has been frankly inspiring.

The umber of people who rallied around his family and friends was nothing short of amazing. So many people jumped in with hugs, tears, and encouragement. One thing did remain—the empty truth that Parker was gone.

The day after Parker died, the church I work for and a local student ministry quickly arranged to have a time of celebration for Parker's life at the church. The room was full of hundreds and hundreds of students, parents, and people concerned for the students in the community.

For what seemed like hours, students shared about their stories of Parker and how he had left an impression on their lives. Everyone said that because of Parker they were a better person. It was a night I don't think I'll ever forget. I had the opportunity to share what I know Parker would have wanted to be shared—that there was a very specific reason why he was the way he was.

Parker Jackson's faith in God transformed him. Parker loved well, laughed often, and encouraged anyone who came in contact with him. Now before you saint him, trust me, Parker was a teenager with regular teenage issues and by far wasn't a perfect human. (Who is?) To his friends though, Parker was the best example of what it means to be a Christian that many had ever seen.

Here's a question I heard a lot from students after Parker's death: "If I died today, would my life have that kind of impact?"

Wow. That's a pretty loaded question, but it's an important one. I had a friend tell me a long time ago, "The only thing that matters when it is all said and done is what's done for Christ. Nothing else remains."

I recently told Parker's parents something that I really meant. There are people who will pass away who are 90 years old whose life impact is nowhere near what God has done in and through Parker's short life and tragic death.

Unfortunately in my years of student ministry I've been around way too much death and tragedy. Every time something like this happens there's a knee-jerk reaction to respond with either a stronger belief in God or a push away from Him. Parker's story drew many closer to Him and I know for many of us it helped us understand what it means to make the most out of the life that we've been given.

I have no idea why God allowed Parker to die that night. What I do know is that God is still in control and wants to use everything to draw us closer to Him.

Let's make this personal for a moment. Has something happened in your life recently that has drawn you closer or caused you to push away from God?

Please know this: There is a God who knows exactly where you are today and what's going on in your life. He created your life for a reason. Your life has a distinct divine purpose. I can guarantee you that Parker had no idea his life would end so suddenly, or that it would have so much impact on others. But God has used tragedy for something amazing—to give others a reason to examine their lives and the meaning of it. If we will see Him in the midst of the storm, God will help us understand the meaning of it all.

The dangerous thing for you and I is to take a horrible event like Parker's death and use it as a reason to hold a grudge against God. If you're hurting and you have questions because of something tragic in your life, go to God with your feelings. Don't run from Him. If you're angry, get angry. If you're shattered, cry to Him. Don't be afraid to unleash all you're feeling on Him—He sees it anyway so there's no need to hide. If you allow your pain and your questioning to lead you to God instead of away from Him, He may not give you answers to your questions, or reasons why the hard things have happened. But He will give you Himself. He promises that He is close to the brokenhearted (Psalm 34:18), and He will walk you through every storm.

My hope for you is that you'll discover that the same God who loved Parker Jackson and changed his life is the same God who wants to do the same in yours.

One of Parker's favorite verses was Philippians 4:13 that says: "I can do all things through Christ who strengthens me."

You did just that, Parker—you lived your life for something much bigger than yourself. Thanks for being an example for all of us. I hope all who come in contact with your life and story will be pointed to the One you lived your life for, buddy. (And I can't wait to have that cup of coffee with you in heaven!)

(For information about a special yearly tournament that has been set up in honor of Parker go here: http://www.legacylacrossecup.com/)

Do I Get a Choice Here?

In school I was an okay student. "Okay" meaning I didn't fail much and was never super honor roll. I think my ADD played into that quite a bit. The peak of my academic career was in 5th grade when I won the school spelling bee. It was pretty much downhill from thar, I mean *there*. I did kill it in rec games in high school—I love me some badminton and bowling. I even took badminton in college. I knew I was in trouble when my mom would call me at college and I'd tell her about the badminton tournament. I remember her asking me once, "Son, are you going to any real classes?" Yeah, that really happened.

There *is* something that I learned the real hard way in college. It's something that my parents and teachers told me while growing up and I never took it to heart. We can put this little nugget under the "had to learn the lesson the hard way" file.

Here it is: "The disciplines you develop when you're young will carry with you into every aspect of your life." Man, that packs a serious punch because the opposite is very, very true. Your lack of discipline will go with you too. Did you hear that? That was the sound of me stepping on my own toes here.

I didn't study much in high school. I did enough to get by. I was the king of last-second test preparation. In my mind I was thinking: "Seriously, there is no need to study now—the Braves are playing!"

And in college, you could always tell when I had something serious to study for—my room was clean. I'd always clean my room instead of studying. You can't really do the "putting work off" thing in college and do well. You can try, but I don't suggest unpacking your bags because you'll be headed home sooner rather than later.

I've talked to so many students about this over the years and I've found that this principle isn't just true academically, it's true spiritually. If you cultivate a lifestyle of studying Scripture when you're young, you'll take that with you.

So many of us live with an "I'll do that later" mentality. Trust an old pro with this one: You might be able to do that for a while, but you won't be able to fully do it well. Sooner or later it'll catch up with you. When it does you'll wish you had made some different choices back in the day. The cool thing is that today is a new day and you can draw a line now and begin to make the right choices and create the disciplines you know you need in your life.

This has happened to me several times in my life. Math is a great example. I always had trouble with math. One of the main reasons is that math is something you have to really study and master to be good at. There is a key word there—study. In other words: Time. Focus. Discipline. I seemingly was always behind in math because I didn't put the time into it that was necessary for me to do well.

We all have a choice. Are we going to let our today set up our tomorrow to be successful or are we going to do nothing and let it… help us fail? I believe that God gave us common sense for a reason. We have the ability to learn on purpose. It's part of our design.

I'm reminded about the time when Jesus said that the wise person builds their foundation on the rock so when the storms came it won't wash away. The person who builds his home on the rock didn't just throw up a place on the beach the easy way. He took the time to build a solid foundation to live off of, knowing that it would sustain him during the good and the bad times.

Our relationship with God is that way. Like math, like building a good house on a solid foundation, it takes time. It takes investment. It takes effort. And the little bits we invest in our relationship with God today will make it deeper tomorrow.

Now you might be thinking, "Okay you're trying to get me to do my homework, right?

Well, sure if that's your issue. I would love for you to think about how you're navigating your life. When I was in college I studied the life of a guy in the Bible named Paul. It changed me. Why? Because Paul is the poster child of changing your life's direction! Paul used to come to towns to kill Christians. Let's just say he wasn't a big fan of the "movement" of Christianity that was taking off around him, so Paul made it his mission to help snuff out the movement. Along his journey Paul had a collision with God and that moment caused him to turn his life around. And the ripples of that decision are still being felt today. God allowed this former Christian killer to write

13 books in His own book— the Bible! Paul had a choice to make about his life. And so do we.

Let's make this specific to your relationship with God. Many of us keep saying that "tomorrow" is the day that we're going to get serious about reading the Bible and really being the person we know God wants us to be. It's easy to let the stuff of everyday life happen and for us to push our walk with God to the side.

That's not how it should be. In fact, your relationship with God should collide with your everyday life. What I mean by that is that in the same way that studying helps you to do well in class, continuing to develop your relationship with God will affect every aspect of who you are and how you live.

This is a math problem I can figure out. The more you put into it, the more you will continue to discover about God and about yourself. The opposite is true as well. Think about this again: what we do today will always affect our tomorrow. If I choose to eat a pizza today and not exercise, I am going to gain weight. If I choose to eat wisely today and exercise, I might even lost some weight! If I choose to study and do what I am supposed to, then I might be prepared for what's ahead. If I don't then I won't be.

The disconnect between God and us starts with our putting off the work of pursuing a personal relationship with Him. Our relationship with God is like any other relationship— it takes time, commitment and trust to develop it.

The choice is yours here, my friend. How do you want to invest your time and energy? The time is now. Make the choice to fully follow the One who deserves your time, focus, and heart.

Choosing to pursue God every day is a choice you will never regret.

Choosing to put your walk with Him off…well that's another story.

DIG DEEPER — PART II

Here are some songs that will help you connect a little more with what you just read. As you listen to them, think about what you just read and how it connect from your ears to your heart.

"Code of the Road" from the Bleach CD, *Static*
"By Your Side" from the Tenth Avenue North CD, *Over and Underneath*
"Bless the Broken Road" from the Rascal Flatts CD, *Feels Like Today*
"Take You Back" from the Jeremy Camp CD *Restored*
"Thanks to You" from the Geoff Moore CD, *Geoff Moore*
"Say Goodbye" from the Skillet CD, *Comatose*
"All Because of Jesus" from the Fee CD, *We Shine*
"Jesus Paid It All" from the Kristian Stanfill CD, *Happy EP*

Here are some verses to check out based on what you read:

Joshua 1:5
Psalm 34:18
Luke 15:11-32
1 Corinthians 10:31
Philippians 4:13
2 Timothy 2:2

Here are some questions to help you think about what you just read:

- What did you like about this section? What connected with you?
- What are some things you've done that might have caused you to wonder if God still loved you?
- How did you get an answer to your wondering? (How did you know if God still loved you or not?)
- How did you relate to "Do I Get a Choice Here"? How does that connect to where you are at in your life?

- Describe your best group of friends. What makes them who they are? Why do you get along with them so well?
- Who are some friends you can form a group with? What is preventing you from having a regular accountability time and time for talking about life?
- As of today, what do you think the legacy of your life is?
- What do you want your legacy to be?
- In "That Night in Alabama," I shared about getting really lost and how I felt. Share a time when you have gotten lost and how you felt.
- Why do we get scared when we realize that we are lost?
- I shared about some embarrassing things that have happened to me. These things have caused me to think about how we can judge people without really knowing them. Have you ever done that? What can you do to help remind yourself that everyone has his or her own struggles?
- What is the danger in judging others? What do you think we can do to not do that?

Let's think about Parker's story for a second. Although he lived only 16 years, Parker has left quite a ripple because of how he lived his life and how he treated others. Let's make the challenge from Parker's life practical for us. If I were to go ask the five closest people in your life what your legacy would be, what would they say?

No matter your answer, I hope you'll be challenged to do your best not just for yourself, but also to do your best for the One who made you. What can you do this week to navigate your life in that direction? Do it!

Like Haitian Vanilla?

Haiti is a quaint little country with great summer days that hit lows of 100 degrees. Good times. The mosquitoes are the size of golf balls. (That would explain all of the massive shots we had to get before we went.) I went to Haiti in high school on a mission trip. We helped build a church for a ministry there. It was a great trip that to this day I'm still learning from.

When I was in Haiti I bought my mom some vanilla from the market. She's a great cook and I knew she'd love the gift. I was told it was the "good stuff." I felt like I was smuggling drugs or something back into the country. Here I was a high school student on a mission trip not sure if it was cool to bring this stuff back to the States. I could practically hear the news headlines: "Teenage missionary caught sneaking vanilla back to the States. Details at eleven." I know, I'm a bad person. Well, I did get through customs and I was able to keep the vanilla. My mom absolutely loved it.

The vanilla I bought lasted mom for years. Why? Because it was the real deal. It was very potent and just a little drop of it went really far. She didn't have to use half as much as she used of the store-bought stuff. The vanilla I brought home was made from the very potent vanilla bean; not by a big manufacturing plant making vanilla flavoring. This was the real thing; true vanilla flavor.

A little bit of some things go a long way.

It's the same way with encouragement. I struggle with that sometimes. I think I'm an encourager by nature. Sometimes I naturally encourage others. Oftentimes I'm not too encouraged by others, mostly because it seems in most of my relationships I'm primarily the encourager.

That often causes me to throw my own little pity party and feel like I'm owed something for all that I do to encourage others. I've had to learn not to seek encouragement from others, but from God alone. You know what? He encourages me all over the place—and He'll do the same for you. He gave us His Word, the Bible, to help light pathways and our lives. His Word will give you what you need when your tank is empty—when you're feeling low on encouragement, give it a try. The Book of John is a great place to start if you want to start reading the Bible. (It gives a great overview of what Christianity is about.)

Some kind words from a friend sure can go a long way though. Are you regularly encouraging other people? Are you being encouraged? Remember that a little bit goes a long way.

But here's the secret: just like Haitian vanilla, it has to be the real deal. It can't be the fake stuff. We all know when someone says something and it seems fake and not genuine. I think fake encouragement does more damage sometimes than not saying anything at all. I had a friend once who was really good at fake encouragement—it was like assembly-line encouragement. I'm not knocking him; it just felt so fake and awkward when he constantly said things that he knew I wanted to hear. I hated that. I honestly just wanted him to tell me what he was really thinking, not some cookie-cutter words. Have you ever felt that way? That you wanted someone to just be gut-level honest? That way if they encouraged you it would really mean something? Wouldn't that be great?

Here's the deal: One day we all have the chance at the ultimate encouragement. The Bible tells us that one day every one of us will stand before God and be held accountable for how we lived our lives while we are here. It tells us He will say one of three things to us: "I never knew you," "You thought you knew Me, but you never did," or "Well done, good and faithful servant."

It could be the moment of the ultimate pat on the back—to have the God of the universe tell you well done for how you served Him in love. Can you imagine what that will be like?

Because I have such a huge desire for encouragement, I'm learning to live my life for God alone. I'm learning that I'll never make everyone happy—heck sometimes I won't make anyone happy. I've learned that as I've aimed my life in the direction of serving God, things like encouragement come as an overflow out of my relationship with Him.

Maybe you find yourself reading this really longing for some encouragement from someone. Maybe you're longing for the day when a friend, parent, or boss says some words you're thirsting for. Maybe you stay awake at night upset at the lack of acknowledgement for the things that you've done with your life.

I wrote those because I've been there...on all of the above. I've been in need of the real thing—true encouragement from a friend.

And much like the Haitian vanilla, a little bit of encouragement definitely goes a long way! I'll finish this chapter with this incredible verse from the Bible: *"May the God who gives endurance and encouragement give you a spirit of unity among yourselves as you follow Christ Jesus" (Romans 15:5).*

Get Help!

One of the greatest lies told to my generation is this: "It's no big deal, no one else will ever know." (You can fill in the blank on what "it" is.)

Ever thought that?

What happened after?

For most guys in our generation the Internet is a buffet of temptation. There's so much stuff that's available. Anyone can access almost anything—and "it's no big deal." If I told you I've never struggled in this area, I'd be lying, because I have. I still do, and from what I've learned from men further down the road than I am, I probably always will. That might be some discouraging news for some of you, but it's a battle we have to face. To deny that the struggle is there and that the battle is taking place is pure ignorance.

I've learned that although my spirit is strong, my flesh can be really, really weak. I need help and badly. The sexual crap available on the Internet is not only destroying our relationships, but our families, churches, and even our self-image.

If you struggle in this area, I want to say something here that you've likely heard before—GET HELP.

I haven't met a guy yet who can handle this completely on his own. So, here's my two-fold advice: Find an accountability group who isn't afraid of asking tough questions. Find a group of friends you trust and commit to meet with each other to help each other make wise choices. Use those times to celebrate the good choices and to help navigate each other away from the bad ones.

The second thing is to make sure that you have a good filter on your computer. I've tried several web filters. They all do different things, but I recommend one that completely blocks any page that has anything potentially dangerous on there. It's better to be safe than sorry!

One of the best filters I've found is Safe Eyes—www.safeeyes.com. I've also recently gone through the 30 days at Pure Online as a way to fill my heart and mind with Biblical truth to defend myself in this fight.(www.pureonline.com) Again, this is not a battle we can fight alone and we all need help and training to fight it well.

This issue doesn't bypass anyone. If you're a human, particularly a guy, lust and impurity is likely something you deal with. God gave us the ability to appreciate beauty, and of course, Satan wants to distort that ability until it puts us in chains. These chains can hold you down and destroy your view of women. These chains can hold you back from chasing the dreams God has for your life because you're tied down to bad habits and not free to pursue the things God has for your life.

So get help. Your future depends on it—seriously.

I'm in a group of guys who've all struggled and we can all see damage that has been caused by our unwise choices. The good thing about our group is the hope that has grown from the grace of God and the promise of forgiveness if we come to God with sincere hearts. We've learned to not dwell on the past, but to cling to the promises of God.

So trust me, friend. Flee. Run away. Find your identity and pleasure in the One who made you. Don't race after finding your identity in things that will never truly fulfill you. Do something wise and run away from the sin that so easy entangles. If you don't run, you're running from God.

While reading this you might be aware that this is the key issue really separating you from a raw, unfiltered relationship with your Creator. Your journey might be moving in a different direction simply because you can't shake this issue—or addiction.

Run to God, my friends. Trust me. Get help from other followers of Him and from God. This struggle will destroy your life—but it doesn't have to. Nothing is ever beyond God's power to redeem, but first, we must take everything to Him.

If you or someone you know needs help from addiction, don't wait to get help. None of us wants to be the person who constantly wonders: "How did I get here?" In many cases that help starts with a friend who is caring enough to have a tough conversation. Don't wait! Get help! You'll be glad you did and you'll find freedom in Christ like you have never dreamed!

Hitch…As a Large, Balding White Guy.

For some strange reason I regularly find myself in the position of giving relationship advice. I'm not sure why. I mean, my dating resume is quite legendary, but still, I'm not sure why God throws me these curve balls every now and then. (The legendary comment is full of sarcasm by the way!) I guess it's because I've read a lot of material and learned a lot about how God views relationships. I've also spent a lot of time helping friends figure out different things that are going on in their relationships.

And here's what's really funny: In the last few years I haven't dated much. There has definitely been the occasional girl that has drawn my interest, but thus far nothing that has made my eyes bulge and my heart melt. It has happened a few times in my life. I am currently batting 0 for 5 on long-distance relationships. No need to go into any names, but there are some special memories of some very special girls that God has put into my life and I am thankful to have crossed paths with each and every one of them. Plus, how awkward would it be if one of you were reading this? Anyway…

As I write this I've just turned 30. To be honest I thought I would be married by now and, heck, maybe even have some little chillin's running around. I do have a hyper dog. My theory is God is using the Murph to prepare me for parenthood. So here I am…not quite where I thought I'd be, and yet I find myself content. That's right, I'm happy. Why? Because I've always tried to be the person that God has called me to be. I honestly think my ministry in the last 10 years would have been severely diluted had I been married or always in a serious relationship. I'm grateful that God has done that. I've been a part of thousands of conversations, opportunities, and quality times with students that I wouldn't trade for anything.

So here I am regularly dispensing advice to people while still single myself. Crazy how God works sometimes isn't it? One thing that gets me excited is the hope of what God has for me. I know who He has called me to be. I have an idea of the kind of person I want to marry, and she's going to have to be one special girl to deal with me. I know that one day, God willing, I might be in the situation to commit my life to another person and I'm no doubt beyond excited about that.

Often after a conversation on this topic I've found myself sitting in a car just asking God, "Why me? Why did You put me in that situation?" Not too long ago I met with a friend and his wife and it became quite a conversation. It was so cool to be able to encourage them and point them in the right direction. They have since given me some great encouragement about our conversation. They told me how it was a true turning point in their walk with God and in their marriage. I just received an email from a student that told me that a discussion we recently had helped him make the wise choice in his relationship and he's really excited about what God is doing. Yet I come home…to my stanky ol' drooling dog that's excited to see me. Great.

God tells us to "Do good as long as it is today." I've learned that the best thing I can do with my life is to trust God with it. He will direct me. He always has. He knows my heart and my desires. I've learned that worrying about things only prevents me from what He has for me at that time.

How does this play out in your life? Do you find yourself being a part of something and wondering why God has you there? Do you find that you have some hopes and dreams that are unmet? Here's some unsolicited advice (although you *are* reading my book)—TRUST.

God is in control. He already knows what's going to happen and very likely He put you in this position for a reason. The answer to what that reason is between you and Him (and sometimes it always remains a mystery). And if in the process of walking through your life you just happen to meet a cool girl that digs students and doesn't mind a big, hairy, drooling dog…holla back at a playa, yo!

Will the Real Jason Carr Please Stand Up?

There is an interesting side to me. I can go do the thing where I'm hanging out with a ton of people and work the crowd and whatnot. I love Sundays at my church when I get a chance to hang out and invest in so many of the leaders and students. I love it when I have the opportunity to go communicate somewhere and hang out. I love going places and running into people I've met along the way and just loving on them. I'm an "extrovert" no doubt. Calling me relational is not a lie. Here's something interesting though—I also love to come home and be left completely alone. This might sound really cheesy, but sometimes silence is my best friend.

This issue is something I've struggled with for a lot of my life—being alone. As you know by now, I'm not married. I've had some great roommates and tons of friends. But at the end of the day, I'm alone. Sometimes I can have my own little pity party about how awful my life is and how much I really need some "real" friends who really care about me for me. (But that's a lie because I have that, I just don't always have it like I think it should be for selfish ol' me!)

I read a quote in a Max Lucado book a long time ago that seriously jabbed me right in the heart. It said this: "Loneliness is not the absence of human contact, it is the absence of intimacy with God." Thanks, Max. I think I have a toe or two left for you to step on. Seriously. Man, that quote put my heart on the tee and just flat hit it off the course.

The reality is that most of the time when I feel alone, I'm really out of touch with my Creator. I begin to think more about what others think about me instead of trusting and believing what God has already said about me. I begin to focus on what I want instead of what I've already been given. So I whine to God about being lonely and I wonder what He's thinking.

Here's the deal, my friend…you're not alone. God *is* there. He knows your needs and will not only put people in your life, but He's always available for you. Right now as you read this He's right there with you. He is waiting for you to acknowledge His presence.

Sometimes I feel like God is way too busy to care about little old me. I know there is famine and sickness in Africa, hurricanes hitting mainland America, and various catastrophes all over the world. (Okay, I had to have some spell check help on the word "catastrophe.") There's part of me that thinks that God is so busy handling all this that He really doesn't have time to consider my issues. I can see it "AIDS in Africa...What? Jason Carr is still single? We need to get on that right now."

Ever felt like God has way too many important things to deal with to get to your little problems? I know I have. And I've found that sometimes our minds can really play some nasty tricks on us. There are times when we need to release these thoughts and focus on the true promises of God.

Here's the hard part: As true as that is, it's not very tangible. That doesn't always help my loneliness. I'm pretty sure that's where faith needs to kick in.

If you're feeling alone, I understand. Life really stinks sometimes and all we want is someone to talk to about it all. We want someone to listen and someone who can relate to what's going on in our life. We want someone who genuinely cares about us. I know. I've thrown some pretty "woe is me" parties over the years.

Sometimes I wonder if the real Jason Carr will ever just stand up and leave the lonely one behind?

Oftentimes I need to know that God is ridiculously aware of my situation and wants to lead my life along His perfect plan and path. If I knew that He was in the middle of my life, and I really trusted that, I'd be okay with the fact that His plan and path isn't always easy. But I don't always trust that, so I struggle.

I wrote this chapter because I think many of us deal with loneliness to a degree. I mean, I have a ton of names in my cell phone and loads of friends on Facebook, but what does that mean? I hope you understand this simple truth: You will never get from others what you can only get from God—a real, raw, unfiltered, unmoving, committed relationship. And there are places in us, in our hearts that only He can fill. Even if we have a billion Facebook friends!

If you find yourself feeling a bit lonely lately, I hope you won't be searching to fill that void only with people, because they're not going to be enough. They're going to let you down. Now, we do need each other, I get that. I'm as big a fan of needing and having others in our lives as anyone you will meet. But there are certain places in our lives that only God can speak to. The great news is, He longs to fill those places, to spill His love over into our hearts. He is ready and more than willing to do that. The catch is, we have to go to Him.

The Big C

I'm writing this in the passenger seat of a car headed south on I-85 towards Florida. It's tough because as ADD as I am, it's hard to type, talk, and watch everything happening, but I'm going to give it a shot!

I have the unbelievable opportunity to help at a retreat this week that's for families with children who have the C word. Yes, that word. It's one word that if you were to hear this word in connection with you or someone you know and love, it most likely means your world is about to come crashing down really quick.

That word is cancer.

In my short time on this planet this disease has had an affect on me. In my time in ministry, I've walked alongside many families dealing with the big C. In my own family the big C has snuck up and taken lives. It's a truly awful thing. One question I've heard a bunch from students over the years is this one: "If God really loves me, than why is my mom sick with cancer?" Insert your own person and sickness or tragedy there. This is such a deep-rooted question.

The truth is this…I don't know. Many scholars and smart people have things to tell you that might be so confusing but might give you a little comfort and make you feel better in the short term. But I don't think anyone can really know. You know why? We're not God.

I do know this—God gave us the freedom to choose wrong and right. Thousands of years ago we (man—aka Adam and Eve) chose wrong. Once that happened, sin entered into this world. And the whole world broke. Along with sin came the curse of death. Sickness came hand-in-hand with death. So now, all we can do is deal with the reality of the fallout that sin caused. And that's a tough pill to swallow.

Today it seems like there are a billion things that you can do, take, or drink to prevent cancer. I'm pretty sure if you don't smoke cigarettes, your chances of getting lung cancer are much less. Rumor is that if you drink a lot of green tea that will help prevent getting it—although it does make you go to the bathroom a lot! One way or another, if you Google "cancer preventative" there are over nine million sites to be found. Nine million! Seriously!

Although scientists are working daily to try and understand the causes and treatments for all of the types of cancer, there isn't a cure-all.

Here's what I do know: Big, difficult stuff like cancer is too much for me to tackle on my own. I need someone to walk me through this. And I've found that if you let Him, God can be a God of comfort. One of the amazing things about God to me is that even though He is God, and He runs the entire universe, He walks with us through our lives. He doesn't stand outside of what He has created, He enters in, He feels, and He walks alongside of us.

The Big C has taken quite a toll on the quality of life of millions. My guess is that everyone that will hold this book in their hands will have been or will be affected by it one way or another. I understand how much it doesn't seem to help the hurt when you hear, "God is in control." It can be confusing to me how a "good God" would allow all this to spread like it has. I also understand that it was us (meaning humankind) that brought sin and evil into this world.

* * * * * * * *

I'm now writing this after just coming home for the week. I can't tell you how amazing it was to spend a week on the beach with families who have children dealing with cancer. The week was a much-needed injection of hope and fun. Although the answers still are few, it's obvious that God was there. So many of the families have stories of finding a deeper faith or a new faith as a result of cancer coming into their lives. Wow.

Chances are at some point in your life you will have to deal with cancer. If not cancer, some other hard thing from this fallen world will cause hurt and pain in your life. It could be a family member, it could be a friend, it could be a co-worker, and it could be you.

The question I would love for you to think about is this: "What then? What happens when something awful happens in your life?"

I hope your answer will point you straight to the One who is still good, still in control, and always interested in your relationship with

Him. And say a prayer today for everyone dealing with cancer. Let's beg God to reveal some new cures, treatment, and hope to those dealing with that today.

* The retreat I wrote about was a Lighthouse Family Retreat. This is a retreat for families who have children with cancer. To learn more about their incredible ministry check out: http://www.lighthouse-familyretreat.org/

DIG DEEPER—DISMOUNT PART III

Here are some songs that will help you connect a little more with what you just read. As you listen to them, think about what you just read and how it connect from your ears to your heart.

"I Want to Love You" from the Todd Fields CD *Free*
"The Best I Can" from The Normals CD *Coming to Life*
"Power of a Moment" from the Chris Rice CD *Short Term Memories*
"The Real" from the nevertheless CD *Live Like We're Alive*
"Dirty Little Secret" from the Pillar CD *Where Do We Go From Here*
"Show Me Love" from the Building 429 CD *Space in Between Us*
"I Am in Love with You" from the Darrell Evans CD *Freedom*
"Missing Love" from the PFR CD *Disappear*

Here are some verses to check out based on what you read:

Psalm 10:17
Psalm 73:23
Romans 12:9
Romans 18:5
Hebrews 3:13
James 3: 9-12

Here are some questions to think about what you just read:

- What does it mean to you to be encouraged?
- How can encouragement be or feel fake?
- What can we do to be authentic in our encouragement of others?
- How do you think most people deal with tragic situations?
- What do you think your life would be like if you totally trusted that God was in control all the time?

- What are some common addictions people can struggle with?
- Why do you think we get addicted to things?
- Why do you think so many guys struggle with pornography?
- When you think about your future, what do you think about marriage?
- Describe a time when you were asked to give advice about something that might have been awkward for you. (Why was it awkward? What did you say?)

This section dealt with some heavy stuff! Chances are as you hold this- you've dealt with some of these things. Take a moment today and look back on your life. What are the struggles that have really held your heart captive? Pray about it. Ask God to free you from the things that are preventing you from living life fully alive in Him!

The Greatest Ending Ever!

I get wrapped up in a good story. I think most of us do. That's why so many of us get wrapped up in movies like *The Lord of the Rings*, *The Matrix*, *Braveheart*, and *Chronicles of Narnia*. They're just phenomenal stories.

In the last few years I've gotten caught up into the TV show *24*. It's incredible story-telling goes in new and crazy directions on a weekly basis. I'll be honest—I think I might be addicted to *24*. I just *love* that show. You never know what might happen. We all have our theories on who the bad guy is or how it might end, but it rarely plays out like we think it will. And I just can't get enough of the mystery of the whole adventure.

If you only watched the last episode of a season of *24* you would successfully ruin the entire season. The 23 episodes before do nothing but set up the last episode. So if you only watch the finale, you're short-sheeting yourself. You miss out on the drama, the character development...the whole story. Plus you miss out on how powerful it is when you see the whole picture.

One of the best stories you'll ever know in your lifetime is the story of your life. God has given you a story. Every day you're adding words to the book of your life. I think when we have major life change it's the beginning of a new chapter. When you graduate high school you're closing one chapter in the story of your life and starting a new one. The same thing is true with all major life events.

So, if I was to read the book of your life, what kind of story is it? Is it sad? Is it hopeful? Is it faith-filled? Is it full of doubt? Would it be full of hate? Maybe it has a bit of regret? How about fun? I hope you have some fun in your book.

Most importantly, what does your book say about how you live your life in light of who God is? Only you and Him know—He sees your heart and every moment of your life. Let me share something about God and His role in your story. God made it so that when He's in our story our lives will be full and adventurous. He made us to be fully alive and only when we are connected to Him cam we get the most out of what He has planned for us.

Here's an important part of God's story. He created our planet and us so that we could have a perfect place to have a relationship with Him. That relationship gives our lives purpose and meaning. There is a problem though, we messed this whole thing up. If you head back to the first book of the Bible Genesis, you will discover that God only gave man one rule. (Don't eat off of a certain tree.)

Well, man did that. And from that point on, that imperfection has caused a gap between man and our Creator. It is a true, but tough part of the story. God is perfect. We are not. Therefore God can't have a relationship with us because of our imperfection. That my friends is what you call the problem—or the tension. And it's a serious problem.

Failure to address this problem will lead to as the Bible calls it "eternal separation from Him." Now listen, I'm not the sharpest knife in the drawer, but I think I'm smart enough to understand that eternity is a LONG time. I think about some classes I had that I thought would never be over. I think about moments stuck in traffic when I had to go to the bathroom wondering if I was ever going to make it. I think about a plane ride once where I got stuck in the middle of two other big guys…and I was miserable. Think about those times that seem like "forever." Now think about this…eternity actually is forever!

Luckily for us, God was not only aware of our problem, but He sent a solution to it. God sent His very Son whose name is Jesus to live with us on Earth. Jesus lived a sinless life (meaning He never did, said, or thought anything wrong.) When He was 33, Jesus paid a debt that you and I could not pay. Jesus hung on a cross and died as payment for the sins of man.

God has offered to reconnect us with Him through a relationship with Christ. If we choose to believe and trust in who Jesus is and what He has done for us, then we can enter into a personal relationship with God. Jesus is the bridge to cross that gap between our sin and God's perfection.

This chapter is titled "The Greatest Ending Ever" for a reason. Unlike 24 or a movie, you don't have to wait until next week to find out the exciting conclusion. You are not going to walk out of the theatre saying "If only they would have done _____." The same

God who has hung the moon and has placed our Sun and Moon in the perfect place to sustain our life offers you and I the chance to jump in on His story. We have a chance to experience a personal relationship with Him.

Think about your life as a story. I believe the most important part of your story is what you believe about God. It will affect every other aspect of your life. The Bible calls God the "author and perfecter of our faith." (*Hebrews 12:2*) So…are you trying to write your story on your own or are you allowing the Lord of All to help you write your story? It's your choice!

Take a moment today and think about the story your life is telling.

Is your story connected or disconnected with the story God is telling in our world?

And the Winner Is…

I enjoy a good ride through the mountains with the windows down and good music playing in the background. One of my absolute favorite places to be in the world is sitting on the beach at night with the breeze blowing and the moon so clear that you think you could throw something at it and hit it. I like flying in planes at night—a lit-up city below you and the stars above you can be some very cool stuff. I've grown quite fond of a really good cup of coffee and there's still something about a good movie with the right company. I love Saturdays in the fall—college football on TV and chili in the kitchen. It's just magical, nothing better. I love me some In and Out burger in California and a little Grey's Papaya in New York City. (Watch out for that Papaya Juice—they aren't kidding about that stuff!) I love eating dinner in Germany and having fresh seafood on the coast is just flat money. I'm as big a fan of music as you'll likely ever meet. The power and effect of music is amazing—it truly is the soundtrack to our lives. I love good conversation with friends. I'm a fan of Christmastime, when for just a short time the world seems to slow down and many recognize there's more to the season than just Santa. (Other than the fact that my Starbucks gets a little too crowded with the seasonal warm-beverage person. Yes, I am a Starbucks snob.) I love my family as nutty as we all are. I think that's what makes us family! I love my dog even if he just started snoring. I love how my friends seem to get me even when I don't get myself. I love a good road trip and enjoy a good belly laugh. I love a good drool-on-the-couch nap when I'm tired. I like it when it's cold in my room but warm under the covers.

I could keep going on and on—the reality is that I love so many things about life. Of all the experiences I've had so far, only one really great thing sticks out as being the best of all of those really great things. There's one thing that is just so much sweeter than the rest.

I love that God uses us to point people to Him.

So many names and faces come to mind. I've had the incredible opportunity to see many friends choose to begin a personal relationship with the one living God for the very first time. I can't think of anything more amazing than being a small part of seeing someone step from a life that's headed towards being separated from God forever to one that is redirected towards heaven to be with Him forever.

You just can't put a price tag on that. Our salvation costs only one thing— Someone's life for ours. It's amazing that God would allow us to be a part of sharing that truth with others. In the bottom of my heart I believe there will never be anything more special or cooler than making a spiritual investment in someone's life.

I've constantly reminded myself of something over the last season in my life. I wrote it and put it over my bedroom doorframe for a while and it says this: "It's worth it."

No matter who, no matter what, when you're acting as the hands and feet of Christ, it's very much, without a doubt, absolutely worth it. How cool would it be to know that every moment of our lives we lived with no regrets? How cool would it be if in heaven, someone comes up to you and shares how you impacted their life, taught him or her about God, and helped them come to know Him? Everyday you have a choice about how you want to live. Everyday you have a decision to make about what you want to value with your time, resources, and talents. How amazing would it be if you used all the things that you are and that you have for something much more important than you?

We all love to do so much with our lives. Go back to the beginning of this chapter and read that ginormous list of things that I love. Take a moment and think about the things you love. What makes your list?

I hope and pray that God would nudge you towards the truth that all those things on your list are there for a reason. And that reason is not just for you. God has given you passions and gifts for things so you can use those to discover Him more deeply and be a mirror to the world for Him.

Now that would be a life worth loving. And that, my friend, is a winner.

I Hate the Mirror

Allow me to share something vulnerable with you. I'm what you could call a little on the heavy side. I've been overweight for what seems like most of my life. Sometimes it bothers me a lot and sometimes it doesn't. I do know that my image of my weight has definitely hurt me from some opportunities that I've had in my life. Someone once told me, "I really want to have you in to speak to our students, but we're not sure about putting you up on stage." Ouch! That cut me really, really deep. So recently, I've been working harder to try to lose weight. Not to please anyone else, but for myself. It has become a moment-by-moment lifestyle for me right now. There are victories, and sadly there are defeats. (Is this starting to feel like an episode of Oprah?)

I've been reading all these different books and investigating all these different plans that help you lose weight. I have tried many—but I've stuck with very few of them. I hate myself for that. I want to one day be a good husband and hopefully a great dad, and I know I won't be able to totally do that if I don't get my weight under control.

There have been some awkward moments being overweight. Flying can be fun—it's always fun putting that seatbelt on without making a scene. (Can you feel the dripping sarcasm?) I've broken my fair share of chairs over the years. I feel awkward sometimes when I go places and people just stare at me. I feel like they're staring at me because of my excess weight. There've been times when I simply haven't gone places because I didn't want to deal with knowing that people are passing opinions about me without even knowing me.

It is stressful being fat.

And the worse thing is that for the most part, it's my fault.

I've learned something about myself recently that I really, really hate. I'm good at getting things started and just awful at finishing sometimes. I have the best of intentions and don't always follow through. I have so many friends I meant to call. I have family I needed to be there for. I have these great ideas for things I'm involved in. And sometimes I just come and go like the ocean's tide. I'm not too happy with that realization. I think for so many years I've moved from one big event to another, never stopping to pause, or think, or really be still. As soon as I leave a conference, a retreat, a big event, I'm thinking about or planning for the next one.

This past summer was different. I had some time off. You know what? I loved it…and I hated it. I had too much time to look in the mirror and see someone that I had begun to miss. I knew that it was time to rediscover the person that God had made me. This has became one of my goals because I think I've finally figured out something important to me—I have to let go and trust God even more with the person He wants me to be. Do I think God wants me to be overweight, stressed out, and live with no margin? Not really, but He is God so I need to realize the wisdom of letting my life be suspended in Him and trusting Him.

One of the things that has absolutely broken my heart lately is discovering how many girls deal with eating disorders. It's crazy, but many solid Christian girls who are walking with God go home from Bible study and make themselves throw up. I remember being at a conference driving home with the girl I worked with. I asked her how the weekend was for her and she started telling me about how these girls wouldn't eat anything because they thought they were already too fat. I was blown away. I couldn't believe that "these girls" would have these issues. They seemed so secure, so innocent, and so in love with God. Yet on the inside they were miserable. I couldn't believe that all these girls I thought were great leaders were dealing with some life-threatening eating disorders.

We all have our hidden secrets don't we? There are things that even those closest to us have no idea about. My secret just happens to be public—all you have to do is look at me. My greatest struggle is openly visible. Other people's struggles may be more hidden. Maybe it's pornography, smoking, drinking, even thoughts of suicide. This reality has taught me a ton about the power of being honest with myself. One of the greatest things for me right now if the ability to know that I am fat and need to lose weight. It has been so freeing to be able to name that, to confess that. It has lifted a huge weight off my shoulders to openly admit that I can't lose weight alone and I need help.

Just recently I really started to understand what a spiritual issue my weight is. Losing weight is a discipline just like reading my Bible and praying. If I can read my Bible and pray and be disciplined that way, but I can't take care of my body when I've been given the chance and ability to, I'm really missing out on what God has for me. For lack of a better way of putting it, I'm not trusting God in every area of my life. This really hurts, to be honest. I really feel like I've let God down a little. I know He is for me and wants me to succeed.

I'm slowly starting to lose weight. I have a long way to go, but by God's grace I'm slowly starting to like the person I'm seeing in the mirror. I've also realized that as a follower of Christ He has told me that He has given me the self-control through His Holy Spirit...I just need to trust Him with that. I need to allow Him to control my motives and my desires. I'm not going to lie to you, this is the hardest thing in my life right now. But hey, if Jesus could conquer death and hell, then I think He has it in Him to help me put the pizza down. What about you? What in your life do you need to trust God with? Be honest!

For a lot of us, the reality is this: We're afraid to talk about what really hurts us because we're afraid of what people think. I understand. I've talked more with others about my weight in the last year than I have my whole life—and it hasn't been easy. Putting my weight out here in this book is part of that. And I've shot straight with you about things for several reasons:

First, I'm starting to realize that here are a lot of people who feel or have felt like I do—left out or judged based on your appearance. Please, please, please know and understand this, friend: God has not left you or forsaken you. God's plan for your life has not taken a break until you drop the weight. You could very well could be like me—God's plan is for you to take your situation and ask Him, "What does this have to do with You?" I hope the answer you get will help you love what you see in the mirror...

Secondly, I'm working through what it means to live my life not worrying about what others think about me, yet still trying to do my best to represent my God. People are always going to judge, I get that. But we can do our best to not add any fuel to the fire.

So, when you look in the mirror what do you see? Are you happy? Are you hiding something so personal that you fear that someone might find out? It's time to look in the mirror and be honest, and then realize that we need each other. I hope you find some hope in your heavenly Father and in the people He puts around you. Now, is it bad that I want to order a pizza after writing this? (Kidding, these carrots are delightful.)

Living Blind

A very odd thing happened to me when I was growing up. (Okay, tons of odd things happened to all of us while we were growing up, but humor me here.) One year I was a pretty good baseball player. I wasn't the best player on the team, but I wasn't the worst. I liked playing baseball a lot; it was my second-favorite sport growing up.

The next year I struck out almost every time I came up to bat. Seriously...I struck out like three-pitches-and-take-a-seat struck out. I became the "easy out" chatter target for the other team. I think some guys would lie down and get a quick rest when it was my turn to bat. It was weird. How do you go from being pretty good to, well, awful?

My parents were trying to figure that out too. We ended up going to the eye doctor to see if there was anything going on in my noggin. Well, there was. We found out that over the last year I had developed a severe astigmatism in my left eye. Basically it's something you can't do much about. I went from having great vision in both eyes to having perfect vision in one eye and being legally blind in the other.

We tried therapy. It didn't help much. We tried glasses. One side of my glasses was just plain glass and the other was as thick as a textbook. Dork, Line 1! They didn't help much either. We tried contacts, but that didn't seem to help a lot.

So basically I live with a mostly blind eye. I can't see out of it, I just focus with it. I can see shapes and colors; I just can't focus in and read anything with it.

Here is what's interesting about this deal. I forget about it all the time. I'm so used to living this way that it really doesn't bother me much anymore. I can drive and live a normal life so it doesn't seem to faze me. I'm so used to living with it that it's really not that big of a deal.

Every now and then it'll come up in conversation and people who don't know will think that I'm lying. It's hilarious to watch how people react when they find out that I'm actually legally blind in one eye.

This disability does not define me, but it does affect me.

Think about that statement for a minute.

What defines you? What affects you?

I've learned more and more in my life how much things affect me. I've also learned a lot about how numb we can be to things after a period of time. Just about every teenager has a "heated discussion" with their parents about movies and music. Most teenagers would say, "I just listen to it for the beat, I don't hear the lyrics." Or, "It's just a funny movie, the nudity doesn't bother me."

Ever said or felt that way? C'mon, be honest now!

Here's the danger in saying or living that way: We get numb to things. We forget that it's even a big deal. Much like I regularly forget that I'm blind in one eye, we can just keep on with things that if we're honest might not be good for us. I've tried to be wiser about the things I watch and listen to as I get older. It's pretty interesting. Because of that, I really am more sensitive when I hear or see something that I know isn't right.

I'm not trying to be legalistic here; I just want to challenge you with something important. Is there something in your life that you know is a problem, but you are turning a blind eye to it?

I hope you're willing to deal with it now, because if you wait to deal with it, it's going to get ugly. I'm not trying to lecture you about how evil music and movies are. In fact, I love both things a lot. I'm just trying to be wise about what I put into my heart and mind. The old adage, "Trash in equals trash out" is still true. If I find myself saying things I know aren't right, it's usually when I'm watching and listening to things that are just that—not right. What we watch and listen to affects how we think. How we think affects how we speak and how we live.

So think about your mental intake for a moment—what's going in and what's going out? I hope that you won't be blind to the truth. What you're putting in your heart and mind might not define you, but it will always affect you.

The things you do and things you think will affect every step of your journey. I hope that you allow those things not to define you, but to affect you in a positive way. I am used to living blind now. It's part of my journey. But it's not all I am. Luckily along the way I've collided with Someone who has defined me.

Thoughts From an Airplane...

I love flying. For some reason being in a plane that's taking off makes me really think about my life. I love getting a window seat and just staring out into the sky. I'm a big guy, so flying can be a bit tight sometimes, but lately I've been really lucky to get upgraded. In fact I'm on a plane trip to Orlando right now sitting in "Business Class." (Thanks, AirTran!) Our flight was supposed to leave before 11 and didn't take off until after midnight. Good times.

I've been doing quite a bit of thinking on airplanes lately. A few months ago I had the chance to go with some students to Bulgaria for Spring Break. That was a great trip. It was my first foreign trip with my iPod. What a difference this little thing makes, especially if you're musically wired like I am. On that trip we left Atlanta, had a few hour layover in Chicago, and then flew to Germany. When we landed in Frankfurt, my battery still had a little juice left. (Shameless plug—if anyone from Apple reads this, I of course am writing this on my MacBook and am a big fan of Apple products. On that note, I pretty much only drink Starbucks Bold coffee lately.)

I've had some incredible conversations on airplanes. I've had my share of awkward moments too. Once I was coming home from Los Angeles and we were waiting to taxi and the guy next to me started talking. He was a really nice guy. He told me, "I hate flying, but with my job I fly at least three to four times a week." When I asked him how he handled it, he said: "What I do now is that I drink too much alcohol and then I sleep the whole flight." Interesting. Before we took off, my boy had around five of those airline alcohol things—that has to be around 50 bucks worth of liquor!—and he flat-out slept the whole flight. We landed, the flight attendant prodded him awake, and he sprang to life like it was no big deal. Amazing! And he does that a few times a week! That guy really made me think about what we will do to sometimes dull the pain in our lives.

On one flight from Atlanta to Denver I had the chance to sit next to a pilot. (He was hopping a flight to fly one back.) That was so interesting. I'm fascinated with things like flying, so I asked him a lot of questions. He was telling me all that was going on and what the captain was doing before and during the flight.

I learned a lot. During the flight he was telling me about how often the captain talks to the tower, how they have this cool navigation system, and even things like how many hours they have to fly. He was telling me about the regulations that are on pilots and how they stretch those limits to the very last mile and minute. (That definitely made me feel really safe.) But seriously, it was so cool to sit next to someone who knew everything about the inner-workings of flying a plane. I know that I probably annoyed him with my billions of questions. At one point people all around us were tossing questions his way.

Honestly, it was really comforting knowing someone right next to you knew exactly what was going on. For some reason even though I fly every now and then, I still get that "I watch too much TV" nervous feeling sometimes about flying. I've seen the shows... I know what happens.

Do you feel that way about your life? A little nervous? Not really sure if your life is on course right now? Are you a little worried if you're going to hit that landing? Pardon me being a bit cheesy here, but let's be honest, sometimes we need a Captain. We need someone to lean on who knows exactly what's going on and can handle the situation. In my life, I've found that Person—it's our heavenly Father.

Consider this: if the Bible is true and God is who He says He is, then He is in complete control. He made you, He knows everything there is to know about you, and He wants to lead you. Unlike an airplane captain, God is completely accessible. He wants to help you with the direction of your life. He knows the route you should take and also the warning signs of when you need to be aware of danger. How is God accessible? He has given us His Word, the Bible, to help us hear from Him and learn more about Him and us. He speaks to us through creation, through people and through prayer. If you have a personal relationship with God, He also speaks to you through His Spirit who dwells in you, called the Holy Spirit. God is in control. That is such a simple statement, but for many of us that's exactly what we need to hear! You might feel like your life is a little out of control right now. Maybe you feel like the emergency light is flashing and you're not sure what to do. Good thing that God is in control, right?

How comforting is it to know that? I hope it makes you even more comfortable than I was that day to Denver with the captain by my side.

DIG DEEPER— PART IV

Here are some songs that will help you connect a little more with what you just read. As you listen to them, think about what you just read and how it connect from your ears to your heart.

"Tunnel" from the Third Day CD *Wherever You Are*
"Beautiful" from the Bethany Dillon CD *Bethany Dillon*
"See You" from the Shaun Groves CD *Twilight*
"Who Am I?" from the Casting Crowns CD *Casting Crowns*
"Story" from the Mainstay CD *Become Who You Are*
"See Through" from the Audio Adrenaline CD *Bloom*
"History" from the Matthew West CD *History*
"Flying Blind" from the Daily Planet CD *Hero*
"If This Is Your Story" from the Alex Nifong CD *The Other Side*

Here are some verses to check out that connect to what you just read:

Psalm 37:37-38
Jeremiah 29:11
Luke 6:42
Romans 8:18
Romans 8:38-39
Philippians 4:8

Here are some questions to help you think about what you just read:

- Share 5 things that you love.
- I shared a big list of things I love in life—did any of those connect with you? Which ones? Why did they connect with you?
- Do you like to know how movies end before you see them? Why or why not?

- How does it make you feel to know that when it comes to our lives and faith, we can know the end of the story?
- How can living as a Christian give us the greatest ending ever?
- What is an area of your life that you struggle with?
- We are all pretty good about making fun of others while being insecure ourselves. Why do you think we do this?
- How did reading what I wrote about my weight make you feel? Why?
- I shared about flying next to a pilot. What did that make you think about?
- Would you rather be in control or let someone else be in control? Why?
- In "Living Blind" I talked about my whacked out eyesight. Thinking about that chapter what defines you? What affects you? What's the difference in the two things?

I'll be honest with you…writing the chapter about my weight was tough. It's tough to be honest with everyone! I've talked with my close friends about this, but I haven't talked to a lot of people about this struggle. Just putting this out there gives me greater accountability in my challenge. It's also peeling back a layer in my life of a personal struggle. It's tough to do that, it really is. Well, you know that because you are a human too. Here's my challenge to you this week. I've taken a big step of faith here to share my struggle with you. I want to encourage you to do the same this week. Quit hiding. Bring your struggle out front and invite your close friends in on your journey to help you out. I'm doing the same thing! Think about that thing in your heart that you are deathly afraid of other people knowing about. Maybe it's time to bring it to light and ask your friends to help you through it. I see a day in my life when I won't hate the mirror as much because I have hope. I hope you can find some hope in your struggles too. It starts with being honest! Take that step this week my friend…

The Dentist

I just got back from the dentist. My mouth hurts and my pride hurts even more. I feel really bad. I have some serious dental issues that'll require another visit and a lot of money. That's exciting. Now I've gotten way better over the years about brushing and actually regularly flossing the ol' choppers, but today wasn't very pleasant.

A few weeks ago I was at a retreat and I chipped a tooth pretty bad. Honestly, once the pain subsided, I didn't really even think about it much. Last week though, I had a horrible pain in my mouth. So I went to the dentist hoping it wasn't going to be too bad.

I hate to say it, but the dentist really is an exposing event. You see if I went to the dentist and he asked me how I was and if I was brushing, then I could just lie to him. But I can't do that because he gets proof of what I've been doing—he takes X-rays, does an exam, and then he knows the condition of my mouth without even asking. And I know that he knows what's going on inside whether I say anything or not.

Here's the deal: God does the same thing. You don't have to say anything or lie to Him, He already knows your condition. How does that make you feel? Sometimes it's cool for me to know that and sometimes it can be really scary at the same time.

When I was in 7th grade, our class trip was to Washington D.C. and I was really excited about going. Mama Carr let it be known that I couldn't go on the trip if my room was dirty, and that I had to have my room perfectly clean for me to go. So I did what most middle school guys do—I did it halfway. I threw crap under my bed and crammed my closets full of all types of stuff—trash, clothes, whatever was in eyesight when you walked by the room. Here's the deal: If you walked by the room, it looked really clean. Upon further inspection, it wasn't all that clean.

While I was gone on the trip, Mama Carr came into my room to hang some laundry up in the closet, and when she opened up the closet door, she got quite the surprise. A ton of stuff just came pouring out like an overflowing volcano. Let's just say that Mom wasn't very happy. She was so mad that she actually wrote me a note when I got home because she couldn't even talk to me. Ouch.

I got in trouble for a few reasons. First, I lied about the truth. I told her that I did something that I actually didn't do. Second, I lost the trust of my mom. Here is the point of this story: It will always come back to you. The short freedom you get from not facing the truth isn't ever worth it.

What's your story? Are you one person on the outside but someone else on the inside? What's your true condition?

What's the condition of your heart? Have you been lying and running from the truth? Have you found yourself wondering how long you'll be able to keep running from the truth? Much like the dentist is aware of the condition of our mouth, God is fully aware of the condition of your heart. Actually, even more so because He is the One who made your heart. He created you and it's Him who actually sustains you. You can't hide from Him. You can run and try, but good luck.

So, how is your heart today? Are you hiding something right now? Are you in denial of what's really going on? Have you numbed the pain so much that you are just used to it? It's time to be honest with yourself and acknowledge what God already knows. It's time to have a heart check-up. Take a moment and ask God to investigate your heart. Ask Him to help you to be fully aware of the condition of your heart. By that I mean, are you angry? Are you upset? Are you nervous? What's taking up space in your heart right now that you might be hiding? It's time to reveal yourself to your Creator. Be honest and allow Him to restore your heart to be what He created it to be, in sync with His.

Even though my mouth is sore, the good thing is that I know what needs to happen to get it in the best shape possible. When I was growing up, I often heard God called "The Great Physician." As much as I hate the dentist, it really is a good feeling to leave when everything is done and you know you're taken care of.

I wonder how many of us really want to be taken care of? I think sometimes we're content just being in bad shape instead of being the best we can be. But just like there's great wisdom in seeing the dentist, there is great wisdom in having a heart check-up from the One who made it.

Life as a Coffee Snob

Over the years I've acquired quite a taste for a really good cup of coffee.

I don't know what that means to you, but to me that means a strong, dark roast of fresh coffee. By fresh coffee I mean freshly ground and pressed coffee. It's the best! (I usually put in a few Splendas in for taste.)

I don't like the medium roast or light roast coffee. To me drinking coffee like that is like drinking brown water. Yes, I have become quite a coffee snob. I just love a great cup of strong, dark roast coffee.

Here is something I've learned about coffee. Everyone has a different idea or thought on it. Some people hate the taste of coffee. Some people just drink it when they need a little pick me up and could care less about the taste. Many people put so much cream and sugar in their coffee that it really doesn't matter what type of coffee it is. Others are incredibly serious about their coffee. I know a friend who goes to Starbucks and orders two of their drinks at a time. One to drink right then and then one for later. They do that every day. That's some serious addiction to the bean!

I have to admit, if I don't have a morning appointment, one of the first things I do when I get to my office is press a fresh cup of coffee. I have a grinder in my office and a can of beans. I grind them up, put them in the press and fill it with hot water. Four minutes later it is a good morning to me! I know that I have issues; you don't need to tell me. But I simply have grown to really like and enjoy a great cup of coffee.

No matter what you think about coffee, I would argue that the way I like it is the best because...well, it's the way that I like it. What is something in your life you really just like? I like my coffee that way I do completely because of personal preference. Many people hate the coffee I like. There are a lot of people who just hate coffee. On the other end, I not only love it, I'm a snob about it!

This is a bit of a jump, but hold on. I've been thinking lately about how we're all wired differently holds true in our walk with God too. We all have unique experiences. Many of us have great churches that help lead us into a relationship with Christ. Some of us don't. Some of us have great music that helps us to connect deeper with God. Some of us think that "Christian" music stinks. Some of us love to hear a good speaker. Some of us hate hearing a speaker. Some of us love the "contemporary church" with the killer lights and sounds. Some prefer a piano and hymnal.

So, is one way right and the other wrong? Am I a bad Christian because I get bored with certain types of churches? Am I wrong that I really like some great musicians who are simply giving their all and rocking out to lead others toward God? Am I wrong because I love it when a church uses creativity to engage the senses and use that to allow God to draw people to Himself?

To some, the answer to that would be yes. For me, the answer is no. Who is right?

One summer when I was on a beach project in college I learned a unique lesson. I was in our room—I shared a room with five other college students—one afternoon after work just listening to some serious 80's guitar rock. (Side note…I grew up with the hair metal and still love it!) One of my roommates came in the room and asked me to turn it off because it wasn't good for him to hear it.

Now I'm sitting there thinking: "What? How can he not want to hear a guitar master just wailing away? Is he stupid? How can he possibly not like this thing I love?" So I asked him why he wanted me to turn it off. His answer kicked me in my soul.

He said: "When I hear that it takes me back to a time in my life when I was making some really bad choices. I've moved on from that and I'm forgiven, but I don't want to be reminded about it. So I just don't want to hear it and be reminded about all the crap I used to do before I met God personally."

Wow. Did you get that? This was a guy who had experienced life change and was convicted of the bad stuff in his life. He was moving from it and wanted to move forward and not be held down by the past.

That summer afternoon I learned what it means to respect someone else's convictions. (A conviction is a convinced conscience about a certain issue.) I knew this guy and his heart. I knew that he loved God and people. I found out that day that he didn't listen to the music I listened to for a serious reason.

I could (and still do!) listen to that music and it doesn't faze me. I listen to it and I'm suddenly 15 again playing air guitar in my basement. Have you ever thought about what it means to respect another believer's convictions? If you don't like coffee, I don't think you're an idiot. If you don't like the coffee I like, that doesn't make you or I stupid, it means that we simply have different tastes that God has given us. Think about these verses from Romans:

> *"For instance, a person who has been around for a while might well be convinced that he can eat anything on the table, while another, with a different background, might assume he should only be a vegetarian and eat accordingly. But since both are guests at Christ's table, wouldn't it be terribly rude if they fell to criticizing what the other ate or didn't eat? God, after all, invited them both to the table. Do you have any business crossing people off the guest list or interfering with God's welcome? If there are corrections to be made or manners to be learned, God can handle that without your help.*
>
> *Or, say, one person thinks that some days should be set aside as holy and another thinks that each day is pretty much like any other. There are good reasons either way. So, each person is free to follow the convictions of conscience.*
>
> *What's important in all this is that if you keep a holy day, keep it for God's sake; if you eat meat, eat it to the glory of God and thank God for prime rib; if you're a vegetarian, eat vegetables to the glory of God and thank God for broccoli. None of us are permitted to insist on our own way in these matters. It's God we are answerable to—all the way from life to death and everything in between—not each other. That's why Jesus lived and died and then lived again: so that he could be our Master across the entire range of life and death, and free us from the petty tyrannies of each other." (Romans 14: 2-9 Message)*

I think about this all the time now when I drink coffee. (Which is a lot!) What does it mean to really enjoy something that others hate? What is it like to respect other believers' convictions that you might not be on the same page with? I was recently in an awkward position with some of my friends who wanted to go see a movie that I just knew I didn't need to see. I've seen enough and heard enough to know that it wasn't wise to be putting that crap in my head. You could say I have a conviction about the stuff I allow into my mind and heart because I see the damage it causes. My friends are believers but they don't share that conviction, so I was left out and didn't go to the movie.

Developing and respecting convictions aren't easy things to do. But—much like a great cup of coffee—you'll enjoy the benefit of it if you find the right place for you and your heart.

I'm not kidding ya, after writing this I really want to go get some coffee. Hmmm, not a bad idea!

That Kid

In 6th grade I wore a size 13 shoe. It would be an understatement to say that I tripped a lot. I had these huge feet and my body didn't match. It was a regular for me to trip if I wasn't watching where I was going. Gravity and myself have never been very good allies. You won't catch the big boy jumping out of any planes on purpose anytime soon. You can go ahead and count on that.

Thinking about this, I remember a very special day when I was in the 8th grade. It was the day that some friends and myself were determined that we were going to break the school record for the 440 relay. I was all hyped up and could vividly see myself running like the wind. (Hey, quit laughing, a guy can dream!) I was just so excited and finally the period that I had PE came. We were on the track stretching and ready to go. I was running the 2nd leg. I watched the lead take off and start running my way. As soon as he was about 10 feet away I started my jog. We made the picture-perfect handoff and I was off to the races…for about 10 feet.

The next thing I remember was my PE coach leaning over me as I was laying sprawled out on the track.

I had tripped over one of my shoelaces and made a direct impact on the track. I knocked myself out for about a minute. How embarrassing is that? I knocked myself out by tripping and doing a head dive into the track. Once I came to, everyone from my class was leaning over behind coach watching the carnage. Then it hit me—my leg hurt.

My whole leg had pieces of track ingrained in it from the trip and fall. Let's just say that I experienced a new kind of pain that day. Some folks helped carry me to the school clinic. (If you're squeamish you might not want to read this part) Here's what the nurse did: She put a huge bowl under my leg, and then she poured a whole bottle of peroxide on it. Owww! I'm pretty sure that half of the school heard my yelp when that happened. Then the psycho school nurse lady took some tweezers and started picking gravel out of my leg. One by one she removed gravel out my leg as I sat and watched.

About an hour later I hobbled into my Spanish class. My whole leg—literally—was bandaged up and I had scratches all over my body. I looked like I had just gotten the tar kicked out of me. Here's the best part: We had a big school dance that afternoon and I was supposed to dance and be hanging out with this girl. Instead I was sitting on the school bleachers with my bandaged leg and a cup of punch watching this girl dance with another guy.

In case you are wondering—I was "that kid."

By "that kid" I mean I was that guy who was just trying hard yet it felt like things never really seemed to go as I planned. I thought it was just me and that I was a goober. And yes, that is true, I was (and am) a goober, but I've since learned that that's part of growing up. Growing up is a series of challenges and mistakes. It's a series of new experiences. It's a discovery of things you love and things you don't. It's an interesting season of life.

Having been in student ministry for a long season now I have some great words for those of you in your teenage years: It's okay! You're not alone. In fact there are thousands of others who feel exactly the way you do right now. The reality is that we don't seem to talk a lot about our mistakes and challenges; we'd prefer to talk about our successes and achievements.

One of the best things about college for me was hanging out with others talking about high school. It didn't take long to realize that we all had awkward moments but didn't talk about it much. We all had faced some challenges and most of us failed in one way or another, but we didn't talk about it much.

Now that I've been given the opportunity to hang out with students one thing I always try to encourage them about is the simple truth that it's okay. You'll make it! Many have come before you and many will come behind you. One of the best things you can do on your journey is to set up the other people who are coming behind you to have the best experience possible. To get there you will need to be honest now and not wait until later.

What is amazing to me is the truth that many of us don't regularly feel like our life really matters. Many of us don't even want to think about leaving a legacy simply because we don't think we could do that. Well, you're wrong!

If God can take someone like me and use my life to do anything good for Him, that's enough to prove that wrong!

We leave a legacy when we're willing to live our lives from something bigger than us. It's in the moment when we realize that we only are given so many days to live and breathe that we truly understand that every day is a gift from God. You can leave a legacy by simply treating people the way you want to be treated. You can leave a legacy by going to extra mile to serve those in and around you. You can leave a legacy by using your talents and gifts to point others to the One who gave you those talents and gifts.

Get it? Leaving a legacy isn't about being the person up front who is always talking. In fact, I think leaving a legacy is more about the person behind the scenes always making sure others have their needs met. God has given you influence for a reason, and it's not for you!

Do you know who has the most influence in the lives of students? It's not necessarily parents. It's not necessarily coaches and teachers. It's not the cool adult person. It's typically other students.

You have one life to live, my friend! I say this a lot, but how cool would it be for generations to come behind you and still be learning about God because He simply put you where He did? Think about it, many years from now you will likely not be in the same situation you are. But...others will be!

What will your legacy be?

If you really want to make something of where you are at in your life right now, I challenge you to think about leaving a legacy that's much bigger and better than yourself. I challenge you to leave a legacy that'll point others to our heavenly Father.

I recently spoke at a meeting for a local high school ministry. The cool thing for me was all the little brothers and sisters who were there because when their older brother or sisters were in high school, they left a legacy. Back in the day they had invested some of their time, talents, and resources to leaving a legacy much bigger than athletic or academic accomplishments. They chose to spiritually invest into the people close to them. They took time to teach those younger than themselves how to follow God. Then those students turned around and taught younger students. So a legacy of following God was passed through entire schools—just because this one group of students at one point decided to follow God. Although many of those students were incredible athletes and even some of them have some awesome things on their resumes, I think one of their greatest legacies will be the spiritual investment they made in others. The ripples of that investment are still being felt today. God used one student to lead another into a relationship with Him, now those students are doing the same thing! All because many years ago someone made a decision to take a step of faith and talk to someone else about God. Many years later they're gone from their high school, yet there are still others hearing about God because they talked to others when they were there. That's quite a legacy isn't it?

One of the coolest feelings I've ever experienced happened in college. I was talking with a friend who went to the same high school I did. He was younger than me, but we hung around the same friends. He wasn't really involved in his faith much in high school, but we were intentional about loving him and trying to point him in the right direction. In college he found that direction in a relationship with Christ. We had lunch one day not too long after he made that decision. He told me "You will never know how much you and your friends influenced me in high school. I don't think I would be following God now if it wasn't for the example of all of you in high school." Wow!

Now is your time. What will your legacy be? The baton has been handed to you. God has you right where you are for a reason! The question for you is what you are going to do with the things God has given you? Think about 2 Timothy 2:2 that says: *"The things you have heard me say in the presence of many witnesses entrust to reliable men who will also be qualified to teach others."* In this verse, Paul is passing the baton of faith onto his legacy—or disciple—Timothy. Lucky for us Timothy picked it up and ran with it. In fact it has been passed on all the way to…us!

Part of my legacy is being "that kid" and I am more than cool with that! I also hope that some of the things I did were and have been a lighthouse to others pointing them toward the only Person worth pointing people to. So, what's your legacy going to be?

The Humbling Fields...

As I write this I'm getting close to breaking the big 3-0. I just watched a bunch of white-haired golfers go by me having a blast with each other as they chase the little white ball around. That's cool. I have so much life to live. Yet I've had the chance to see and be a part of some really cool things, and travel to some really cool places.

The other day, I had a really interesting conversation with a friend. We're about the same age. He is married and has a kid on the way. He has made a pretty good living at his job. They have a nice house and nice cars. From the outside looking in, they're living the American dream. Yet he said he was jealous of me. What? Jealous of me? I was thinking that I was jealous of him!

I'm not married, I don't have much money to my name, my car is falling apart, and I've spent the better part of my adult life working in student ministry. (I don't write that to make myself sound sad, I love my life!) He said he was jealous of how I have lived life following where God has led and investing in students. To be honest, I've never thought about it that way.

I remember a night many years ago when I was still in college. I was sitting on the beach and looking up at the stars and telling God, "Here I am, send me." As I've studied the Scriptures the apostle Paul talks about when he gave his life to God, he ultimately submitted himself to his King. He talks a lot about the fact that his life is no longer his, that he had given control of it over to the One that made it. At the end of the day, the statement of Paul's life was simply this: "You are my Master and I am Yours. Have Your own way, Lord." That's how I felt that night. God, my life is Yours. Do what You will. It reminds me of the scene in *The Count of Monte Cristo* where Count Mondego's son says to the robbers in Rome: "Do your worst." From the moment I told God to have His way, He has done just that. And it has been quite a journey.

I have some breaking news for you: You will die. Sorry to be morbid, but it's true. You and I both are frail. Death is a tragic reality...or is it? It has been said that after you die, "you can't take it with you." Meaning, nothing that you own on this earth—no material possession—is going with you to heaven. It doesn't matter what kind of car you drove on earth, what matters is what you did for your King.

I have the great opportunity and at the same time I struggle to live in a very interesting city. There's a lot of wealth around me. In fact the zip code I live in has one of the highest incomes per-capita than any other zip codes in the entire United States, and therefore the world. It's interesting when I show up to a student meeting and I drive the worst, most beat-up car there. Many of the students in this area get a new $40,000 SUV when they turn 16. Yet sometimes I martyr myself thinking that I've spent over 10 years working in student ministry and I can't afford to get my car fixed, much less get the car I really want. Gosh, that sounds really sad doesn't it? (Ummm, that's sarcasm!)

After thoughts like that, this thought always come to my mind: "What do I deserve?"

The honest answer is nothing. I deserve nothing. The only thing I really deserve in this life is something I've been saved from—and that's separation from my Maker. I don't deserve to drive an SUV or to drink an expensive cup of coffee. (Fill in what you struggle with there!) By God's grace and mercy I've been given so much more than I deserve.

I vividly remember being in high school and going on a mission trip to Haiti. Before I left I got in an argument with my mom at the store because I wanted the expensive "cool" shampoo that all the cool kids were using. She wanted to buy the 99 cents value shampoo. She won. I was mad.

That's right—the teenage missionary was mad at his mom at the grocery store over shampoo. What a stud I was. Seriously…when we were in Haiti we went to the black market and they had soap. *Wow*, you might be thinking, *soap*. You walk into Wal-Mart and it seems like there are hundreds of choices for soap. At the black market in Haiti there was just plain white soap. Not the "fresh mountain springs rainfall lilac" soap…just plain, white, clean-you-up soap. While I was at the market in Haiti, I remembered the shampoo incident. I was practically knocked over by my selfishness.

In Romania we spent money to buy toilet paper. The stuff that the hotel had was, shall we say, a little rough. So we spent some of the money that people gave to support our ministry on toilet paper. That's right—the Americans are here and we only wipe with the good stuff, people! We bought some "nicer" TP. It wasn't too nice, but it was nicer than the sandpaper supplied by the hotel. Come to think of it...maybe that's why some of the folks in Romania are so moody—they have to wipe with that stuff regularly. So we had our own pink TP. (I called the bathroom in Romania the Pink Paper Processing Plant.)

In hindsight (no pun intended), we're sometimes so selfish that it's just funny.

In Bulgaria we stayed in a hotel that had bathrooms in each of the rooms. That's called a luxury, friend. I'm blown away at how comfortable I live and even what I've come to expect is "normal." I remember a student in Bulgaria telling me how he wished so much that he could afford to get a guitar and that's all he wanted in the world. It made me feel really awkward that back in Atlanta I had a basement full of un-played guitars.

When I've interacted with Christians overseas their faith astounds me. In Haiti the worship was nothing short of amazing. The people lived in nasty huts. They had nothing. Yet they were (and are) so passionately in love with God they gave it back to Him in worship. I was stunned. In my thoughts I was thinking: "They should be mad at God for living here and being dealt the cards they have been." But that's not how they think. Instead, they recognized that God had rescued them and given them hope. They loved to worship and thank Him for who He was. Wow. Yet I want more stuff.

This brings up an interesting question...If I'm really honest with myself, am I really thankful for all that I have? Am I grateful for running water? In many ways we've become a fairly ungrateful society. When was the last time you watched a commercial and someone said: "You don't need to buy our product. Your life is fine." Can you imagine what it would be like if our culture supported the thought of always being grateful, even when you don't have what you think you need?

I think we all need to spend some time in the humbling fields! Let's not forget about what we deserve and get caught up in what we think we need. It's a harsh reality when we realize how much we love stuff. Let's not fall too much in love with stuff because as you've likely heard before...you can't take it with you! (Talking about all the stuff)

What we do take with us is our soul.

Let's not become so numb that we get caught up in what we think we need. It's time for us to take a walk through the humbling fields and remember who God is and who we are.

Take a moment and think about all the "stuff" that you really want right now.

Think about what you deserve right now based on your life.

Check this out: "He will not always accuse, nor will he harbor his anger forever; he does not treat us as our sins deserve or repay us according to our iniquities. For as high as the heavens are above the earth, so great is his love for those who fear him." (*Psalm 103:9-11*)

Humbled yet? Listen, I'm not trying to make you feel guilty here. It's just tough when we realize who we are and who God is. He is perfect. We are not. And when He tries to connect with us it can be quite the collision!

Time to Move On

Join me in a cool moment from a few years ago...

It's late. Let me explain that—it's late for me. I'm a night person; I'm naturally up later than most. (Except for my rock star roommate who makes me feel somewhat normal.) I've become a huge fan of the every-now-and-then mid/late afternoon nap when it's available! There is nothing like a good drool-on–the-sofa power nap. Back to the time—it's late; in fact it's closer to morning than it is night. *Why is he up?* you might be asking. Good question!

I'm up because I've been up all night thinking, and I can't stop my mind. It started about midnight when I walked the Murph outside to take care of his before-bed business. It's a nice night tonight, summer is getting really close and you can feel it starting to creep in. I thought I would just sit out here for a while and stare at the stars. My roommates are out of town playing some rock-and-roll somewhere, so it's just the dog and I tonight. Actually it's just me, the Murph, a great cup of coffee, and some lightning bugs.

I ended up making coffee. Not decaf which I usually make at night, but the real deal. And here I am a few hours later, thinking. I'm thinking about this book a little, but more importantly I'm thinking about the massive amount of change that's going on in my life right now. My life is changing in a pretty massive way. I don't know what's next, yet I know God is calling me to move on. Have you ever been in a situation like that? It's time to move on, yet the future is unknown?

I've spent the last ten years on staff full-time with a great student ministry. It has been my life's passion—reaching out to students with the love and hope that only comes from a personal relationship with God. This is my identity to many who know me and it's interesting to think that's changing.

It's still my passion, except I just know that I need to move on. Let me explain—this past school year has been one of our best ever. We've had a ton of students involved in our weekly meeting, many plugged into small groups, and a herd of students drawing a line and making a stand for their faith on their campus. It has been pretty dang cool. Except in the midst of it, I've had this simple feeling like I was on my last lap of this race.

I remember it so well because it happened just a few months ago. I was really, really struggling with this feeling that it might be time to move on. It has been scary—and to be honest—really faith testing.

Over the years I've been blessed enough to have some great people who are further down the road than I am make an investment in my life. When this was going on I knew I needed to talk with some of them. A little over a month I ago I pulled in to meet one of those guys at a coffee shop. At this point I was pretty beat up emotionally and spiritually over this. (This has been my life's work—it's hard to walk away from it!)

I knew what I needed to do, and just didn't have the guts to say or do it—yet. I shared my heart with him and he just listened and asked me questions. He finally stated the obvious: "It sounds like you know what you should do, it's just a matter of you having the faith to step up and do it." Simple words that just flat opened my heart and released me. It was such an incredible feeling—to be able to let go of the things that are troubling you and let God take it.

Very slowly I began to tell those close to me what was going on in my heart and ask for their prayers and support. Eventually I got the support and release of my ministry leadership. I then began to tell all of the incredible friends who have come alongside and supported my ministry financially and prayerfully over the years. That was exciting and tough at the same time—I've been blessed with some amazing partners who have really believed in what God has done in and through me over the years.

A few weeks ago I talked with my staff team that I've given leadership to and they were supportive. And then came tonight...I told the students at our SV Meeting that I was going to be leaving staff. Wow. It was a tough thing to do.

Can I tell you this was one of the hardest talks I've ever done? I was trying so hard not to cry! Let me be honest here with you—the big guy cried. On the way to the meeting tonight all the faces came to mind of the thousands of students I've had the opportunity to meet over the years. Someone asked me to count and I discovered that I've had the opportunity to be a part of over 400 Monday night meetings, over 700 small groups, and countless conferences and trips.

Over this period I discovered that one very faithful God and one goofy guy was evidently a recipe for some cool things. I'm not going to lie to you; I just started crying while I was driving on the way there. It all came to a head. I'm so thankful for all that God has done and for allowing me the chance to be a part of it. It's still quite overwhelming how good God is. Honestly, I'm a simple nobody. I'm nothing special. I have no clue why God has given me all the opportunities He has, because I haven't deserved one of them. I've messed up so many of them I don't know why He is still for me.

So here I am, a few hours after the meeting sitting on my back porch just thinking about all this. I'm thinking about God's faithfulness, about how His ways are always perfect and mine are mostly stupid and misguided. I'm thinking about how much I'm going to miss these students yet I know what God is calling me toward. God has been so faithful, and I have no reason to doubt that He won't continue to be.

I've learned some serious lessons in the midst of this season. First is this: When you know God is asking you to do something, it's right to listen and follow. When you hear and don't follow, life can get quite complicated. Secondly (and I say this very proudly) it's cool to be able to look back on this past season on my life and be proud of what God did. I'm so thankful to be on the journey to live a life that I hope glorifies God. It's very humbling to serve God, but quite the fulfilling lifestyle to trust Him with everything.

(This was written two years later.)

So it has been almost two years since I wrote that. Wow. Just reading that makes me think back to that night. I still remember it fondly as one of the best nights of my life. As I sat there I laughed, I cried, I thought, and I became more and more grateful that God wants to use me. It's still overwhelming to me.

As you hold this book I hope you're picking up a theme here. God wants to use you. If He can use a goober like me to at least attempt something for Him, then who knows what He might want to do through your life!

In the last two years I've kept close to that ministry. I've continued to lead a small group and even get a chance to hang out and speak there every now and then. The coolest part of it for me is it's still going on years after God used some others and myself to get it started. It's a constant reminder of how big God is. I don't want to ever forget that.

God has also opened so many doors for me that I think wouldn't have been opened had He not given me the opportunity to do what He had me do for that great season in my life. It's true—one thing really does lead to another. I hope wherever you are today; you understand your part in God's story, because He has you where you are for a reason.

DIG DEEPER—PART V

Here are some songs that will help you connect a little more with what you just read. As you listen to them, think about what you just read and how it connect from your ears to your heart.

"Legacy" from the Nichole Nordeman CD *Live at the Door*
"From the Inside Out" from the Hillsong United CD *United We Stand*
"Inside Outside" from the Delirious? CD *World Service*
"Legacy" from the Sanctus Real CD *We Need Each Other*
"Moving on Faith" from the Jadon Lavik CD *Moving on Faith*
"Dare You to Move" from the Switchfoot CD *The Beautiful Letdown*
"One Real Thing" from the Skillet CD *Alien Youth*
"Worlds Apart" from the Jars of Clay CD *Furthermore: From the Studio, From the Stage*
"I Will Go" from the Starfield CD *I Will Go*
"I'll Give" from the Smalltown Poets CD *Smalltown Poets*
"Coffee Song" from the Jars Of Clay CD *The Essential Jars Of Clay*

Here are some verses to check out that connect to what you just read:

Psalm 103:9-11
Proverbs 21:2
Matthew 13:15
Matthew 28:18-20
Romans 14:2-9
Romans 14:22-25
2 Timothy 2:2
2 Timothy 3:10-17

Here are some questions to think about what you just read:

- How do you think the rest of the world is different from what you are used to?
- Why do you think motivates people to go on mission trips?
- How can you be a part of working in "the humbling fields?"
- What do you think about the chapter about the dentist?
- I wrote about how the dentist can see what's happening no matter how we try to hide it. How did you connect with that?
- What does it mean to you to have a conviction about something?
- Share some convictions that you have developed in your life.
- What does it mean to you to respect another believer's convictions?
- Why is it hard to respect another believer's convictions?
- What is the toughest decision you have ever had to make?
- How did you make the decision? Who did you talk to? How did you come to the decision that you made?
- How did you relate to me writing about being "that kid?"
- Share a story about something awkward or embarrassing that happened when you were a kid. (Because we all have them!)
- Once again! What do you want your legacy to be? What can you do to navigate your life in that direction?

This section hits on a lot of issues didn't it? At this point in the book I hope you see where we are going. We are taking a look at the things in our everyday life and learning from them. *God is in the midst of everything in our lives.* I think if we take time to look back in our past and learn from it, then we will be prepared to walk wisely in our days ahead.

I wrote about being "that kid" in this section, which was funny to think about! I wrote about my trip to the dentist that made me think about how much I think I am hiding from God. I also wrote about some trips I've had the chance to go on and hang out with some students in different countries. And of course, this section includes the life-changing chapter on my beloved coffee bean. (OK, life changing?) These are all things from my everyday life. When we look at these things from the filter of colliding with an incredible God, there is much to learn!

I want to encourage you to do something that might be interesting for you: put this book down and go sit and think. Think about the journey of your life. Think about the good, the bad, the not so good and the great. Think about the highs and lows.

Now, think about what God wants to teach you from those things. There is a lot there I know. You might want to write it down to help you process it all, but I guarantee you that your very life is a wealth of information and wisdom about our God. Sometimes it just takes us stopping and looking back to learn from it. I promise you if you do that you will not only learn from what's behind you, but also be ready to take on whatever God might have ahead of you!

Start with thinking about 3-5 things that have been important moments in your life. What did you learn about God from that? What was God trying to tell you about who He is from what you have been through?

Take some time and dismount my friend. Enjoy the journey!

Be Recognized: Intro

Who are you? If someone were to ask you who you are, what would you say? Would you say what activities you're involved in? Would you say what faith you believe in? How would you define who you are?

As we land on the last part of our time together, we have a really important question to answer. Who are we? How do we know who we really are?

To be recognized basically means to be identified or to be acknowledged. Don't you love it when you go somewhere and you run into someone you know? It's a great feeling when you're recognized!

I've been on a pretty random streak of being recognized lately and not even at home. I was in San Diego for a trip with our church and randomly ran into someone. (At a Starbucks. Shocking, I know.) I was in Florida on my way to our church camp and stopped at a gas station and ran into an old college friend. I just got a random MySpace message from someone from high school who heard my name on the radio for an event I was speaking at. (Which by the way, it's still weird to think that my name was on the radio. What a crazy world we live in!) They Googled my name and next thing you know, they contacted me. I was at a Starbucks (again, shocking) in Alabama and ran into a guy I knew when he was in high school. I gotta tell you, it's a really good feeling when someone knows who you are and acknowledges it.

On the other side, sometimes it can be embarrassing to be recognized. Like the time when someone said, "Hey, aren't you that guy that spoke at FCA with your fly down?" Yep. We've all been there. All of our lives have a resume that has some kind of recognizable mistake on it.

I don't write those things to share about all these places I've been. I write them to tell you that no matter where you go, you're always who you are. No matter where you go, you're always going to represent who you are. You can lie as much as you want, but you know the truth!

So who are you? On the inside who are you? Not what people think of you, but who you know you really are!

It's an important question. As we'll see in the following chapters, I think it's one of the most important questions you'll ever answer. It's time that you recognize the truth of who you are and who God is on your journey!

Mixed Messages

Let me ask the question again: Who are you?

That's a great question and for many of us it's a really hard question to honestly answer. It's not that we're unaware of our name or the basics of our identity; it's that we live in a world and culture that's hurling things at us at a rapid pace telling us who we should be.

We're being told that if you're a guy and if you wear a certain type of body spray then half-naked girls will charge after you. If you follow sports then you could get the thought that if you have fame and a lot of money you can do whatever you want. If you're into fashion then certain TV stations, shows, magazines, and websites seem to dictate what's cool. You might think that if you're not enlisted in the Abercrombie Army then you're a fashion loser. (Or you might think that because I wrote the name Abercrombie that I'm a loser.) We all have opinions about identity. But how much of those things have caused you to rethink who you are?

I'll always remember a pair of shoes my mom bought me in middle school. I thought they were pretty cool. She got them at K-Mart and they had a Georgia Bulldog on the side of them. The shoes were red and white and being a Bulldog fan I thought they were cool. The next day in science class a few people made fun of my shoes saying that they were cheap and crappy shoes. It didn't help that a few girls were in on the hazing. Because of that one time, I hated those shoes. In hindsight, they were pretty dang cool but I let someone else tell me if I should wear them or not.

I've learned that unfortunately I try to find myself in things that don't really matter. I've traveled enough overseas to understand that an orphan in Romania isn't going to avoid you because you aren't wearing American Eagle. A homeless person downtown isn't going to walk away from you because your purse is from Target. Yet many of us won't walk out our front doors if we don't think we represent what we think is important not only to us, but to others as well.

I can't tell you how many different types of soap and deodorant I've bought because the commercial lured me in. I've tried Lord knows how many special sandwiches or deals at restaurants because of the cool commercial. Haven't you? C'mon, there is a reason so many people watch the Super Bowl—to see what's next in commercial world. All these things are feeding us messages about what the world says should be important to us. The question is how much should we really be listening?

I'm going to write down a few names of companies and as you read them, think about what message they might be sending to you:

Nike
Axe
Starbucks (I had to)
Apple
Taco Bell
Mercedes
Under Armour
McDonalds
Ford
Abercrombie & Fitch
Sears
Coca-Cola
Old Navy
Budweiser
Pepsi
The church

There is a great chance that as soon as you saw the name, you had an instant thought of what you think about the brand. You immediately defined them as something. Guess what? The same thing happens to you. If you ask me about my friend Joe I will quickly tell you something about him. Same thing about Darren, Joe, George, Sean, Justin and, well, you get the picture. We all have a message we're sending out to the world. For many of us, we're not sending out the best message by the way we live our lives. This might be because we're allowing ourselves to be defined by shallow things of this world like a shoe company. Not to be stupid here, but do your shoes really define you? I submit that you are much deeper than looks and skills. You have a heart and in that heart you have an identity.

We really do need to reset our identity regularly because it's so easy to think of ourselves in a way that's not really that important or healthy. Abercrombie is just a brand, a marketing ploy. Don't let it define more than that. If you want to know who you are, ask your Creator. Let Him make that call. After all, He made you. And that is a message that comes in loud and clear!

Pieces of Me

I was recently at a conference and the speaker encouraged everyone to take a moment and write down everything that came to mind about "who I am." So do that—take a moment and think about (and maybe even write down) some of the things that make up who you are.

Here is some of my list:

I am a son
I am a brother
I am a student
I am an employee
I am a co-worker
I am a learner
I am a follower of Christ
I am stubborn
I would like some coffee right now. (Oops…that's just what's on my mind!)
I am a dog owner
I am a car owner
I am a homeowner
I like music
I like college football
I love movies
I love hanging out with the guys in my small group
I like hanging out with my friends
I have a short attention span
I like to think
I am not always a good follower
I like to challenge
I like to read
I love watching my favorite movies and TV shows over and over again
I like to cook
I like to eat
I like to travel, but like coming home even more

I like dreaming
I like truth
I don't like constant negativity
I like freedom
I like forgiveness and grace

That's just a partial version of my list. It was amazing when I took a moment to think about all the things that make up who I am. It's still amazing to look at this list and realize all the things that make up all the parts of who I am.

Have you made your list yet?

Do it.... Really! You should do it...

I'm waiting...

Still waiting...

Okay, good! Were you amazed when you made your list? It's pretty crazy to discover all the pieces that make up the puzzle that's uniquely you.

The thing that's interesting about all this is that not one of those things completely defines me. Sure, I'm a son to my parents, but I'm much more than that. Sure, I love the power of music, but that's not all I am. Yes, I am a Christian. But what does that really mean to be a Christian? Does that mean I have to wear certain things and say certain words? There are many things that make up who I am, but only one thing will completely define me, and that is this: who I know I am in my heart.

How do you really know who you are in your heart? I'm no rocket scientist, but I think the best way to know our heart is to go to the One who made it. So let's read some words from the book that He has given us:

"O LORD, you have searched me and you know me. You know when I sit and when I rise; you perceive my thoughts from afar. You discern my going out and my lying down; you are familiar with all my ways... For you created my inmost being; you knit me together in my mother's womb" (Psalm 130: 1-3, 13).

God knows everything about you, my friend. He not only knows every part of your list, He knows everything…every single little thing. He created you. **You are a priceless person and He created you to know Him personally**. You are incredibly valuable to Him—in fact, you're worth His Son.

I think if we could peel back our hearts one of two things would be true. Either we fully understand and believe that God values us, or we don't. If we believe that God loves us, we'll believe what He says is true about us. If we don't believe that we are loved by Him, that we are valued by Him, then we'll look elsewhere for that love and value.

Here's the sad catch: If we build any parts of our identity on something different than who God says we are, it will crumble.

I know, that's tough to read. But if we define ourselves by anything besides what God says is true about us, those things will eventually crumble. There is never enough money. Relationships and people change. Life happens. As life happens things will change and seasons will fade in and out. The only thing that will be the rock for you to build your life on is your relationship with God.

I've had times in my life when I think my identity was based on things in my life. It might have been something that happened in sports. It might have been that girl. It might have been that rockin' car I drove in high school. (Ummm…ok, maybe not that.) You and I are great at this…we take a singular piece of our life and we build the rest of our lives around it. The danger is that piece will one day crumble.

So do yourself a favor and take stock today. Where is your identity coming from? Are you building your life on a relationship with the One who will always be there or are you building your life on something sandy that will one day crumble?

Please understand this…I'm not saying that you shouldn't pursue all the pieces of your life to be the best person God has you here to be. Just don't build your life around things that aren't completely built on God. Take it from someone who has watch things crumble around him time after time—it's not worth it!

Fed Up?

Today has been a rough day. It has been one of those days when you become fully aware of just how much the world can really suck sometimes. On my calendar, today looked awesome. I had some meetings scheduled with some good friends to talk about several things going on. Every time I left a meeting today my heart just got heavier and heavier.

I have a good friend who is having some serious problems with addiction. It's tearing him apart and he knows it. He just can't get away from it.

I know a student who is just really struggling to find his way in the world. He told me today that he hates his parents (because they actually give him boundaries), hates that none of his friends really understand him, and is pretty much addicted to porn.

I met with another student and leader today. The student's parents are getting a divorce because the dad has been having an affair. The leader is trying to figure out what to say to the student in the midst of crazy frustration.

In my email inbox today was a message from a parent whose son got physically mad last night because they told them they are not going to buy him a car when he turns 16. He threw some things and broke them and cussed his parents out.

I got a call on my way home today from a friend telling me that a mutual friend of ours had crossed a really unwise moral line with his girlfriend. It's okay though because they "love each other."

Have you ever had those moments when you just see how broken and messed up our world is? Have you ever been just frustrated by all the crap that's not only happening around us, but many times *in* us?

That's been my day. I wish I could tell you that this is the only day like this, but I've had many and know that you have or will have them too.

It would be really easy to be discouraged when we face issues that show our sin. It can be easy to get mad at God or even choose to run from Him when things don't go our way or life throws you a curve ball.

But you can't. Well, you can, but let me encourage you why you need to stay in the ring and keep fighting.

It's pretty simple. Your Creator has *never* given up on you. Think about all the things you've done wrong in comparison to God's perfection. How many questionable actions, words, or thoughts have you had? If I even tried to count I'm pretty sure we'd have to invent some higher numbers. Serious.

Yet, even though we were still sinners, Christ died for us. He knew of our crap. He was fully aware of how awful and messed up our world is. And He still chose to stay in the fight and rescue us. His love for us compelled Him.

There is hope in Christ.

I have no idea what might be going on in your life right now. One thing I do know is that you are a flesh-and-blood human being. That means you are likely constantly chasing after happiness and acceptance. When you don't get those things, you will look for them in something else. When you don't get them like you think you should, you will search for it. And make no mistake, my friend, you and I are great at looking for our acceptance and identity in the "stuff of this world."

But all that stuff will eventually leave you empty and broken. You will get fed up and start the process all over again of looking for what makes you happy. I've done it so many times it's embarrassing. I think of all the times I placed my identity in accomplishments or some type of success. I also think of all the times I felt empty because of the lack of those things. I remember the time I pulled up to speak at an event and the students made fun of my car. I felt like a loser. Here I was showing up to speak about God and I wasn't fully confidant in who I was because I let some snot-nose kids tell me my car was uncool. Wow.

My guess is since you're a red-blooded human you wrestle with this. You see the junk of this world and the junk in your own heart and you can get fed up. It's going to happen. Here is the kicker: Your response to the reality of the sin of this world will lead to the next season of your life.

If you are cool with all the sin of the world, you might just jump in and join the party. If your own sin and the sin of others sickens you, it will move you to action. One way or another, you will do something when you come face-to-face with the crap of this world. What you choose to do will pave the path for the next season in your life.

Where are you on your journey of life? Are you happy with where you are? Have you wandered off because you've gotten so okay with the junk of this world that you don't even really notice it much? Are you in tune with God's heart so that your sin and the sin of others breaks you? Are you fed up with the reality of your sin yet?

Thinking about this reminds me of a passage of Scripture. It's found in Proverbs chapter 3 verses 5 and 6. It says this: *"Trust in the LORD with all your heart and lean not on your own understanding; in all your ways acknowledge him, and he will make your paths straight."*

As you see everything going on in and around you, our part of this journey is to trust that God is who He says He is and that He can do what He says He can do. There is a lot involved in trust. It's a two-way street. Trust takes belief in something. Trust takes action. Trust takes hope.

As you travel on your journey of life, you will no doubt have to make a decision about sin. Are you going to run away from it, or run toward it? I pray that you'll be so fed up by it that you'll run from sin and sprint into the holy arms of the only One who can completely satisfy your every want and need. I hope you will choose to trust in Christ. You and I have done enough to make Him fed up, yet He still chose to sacrifice Himself so that we can truly live.

The Greatest Moment of Recognition Ever

A lot of people throughout human history have asked God: "Who are You?"

To answer that question I want to take you back in the day. I'm not sure what back in the day means to you, but in this context back in the day is well over 2,000 years ago. Here's why: I believe that the greatest impression that has ever been made since the creation of this planet we live on was actually made quite some time ago! The cool thing is that this moment in time still affects us all today.

It's the greatest moment in human history.

Being recognized is a funny thing—it might last a few seconds or it can last for eternity. I believe that the greatest impression ever made in history was made over 2,000 years ago on a hill called Calvary. On this hill we find a loving Man who was completely sinless yet was beaten and bruised and killed. Why was He killed? In the spiritual realm He was willingly paying a debt that we could never pay. This debt? Our sin. Sin is a churchy word, but it means our imperfections, things that you and I have done that are wrong.

Ever lied? Cussed? Stolen something? Cheated? Gossiped? Struggled with lust? Envied someone or something? Been jealous? Disrespected your parents?

In the Bible in Romans 3:23 it says: *"All have sinned and fallen short of the glory of God."* You see, God is completely perfect. God can have nothing to do with sin. He is that perfect. In Genesis, the first book of the Bible, we see that God created man to know Him. But then, we sinned. And our sin, that imperfection, can't be in the presence of God who is holy and perfect. So our sin eternally separated us from having a relationship with the One who created us. Let's just be honest, this sucks. What this means is that all the mistakes in my life have caused me to be separated from God forever. You're probably thinking, "Well thanks for the happy ending to the book," right? Well, read on, friend.

But God sent a solution to the problem. He wasn't content to have the people that He loves separated from Him. So He sent His Son, Jesus Christ, to Earth. Jesus came to earth to live a perfect life and then die. Because in the way God set up the universe, sin could only be paid for by the blood of an innocent creature. It may sound weird, but when God made the universe, that's how He set it up. He made the world and the rules it operates by and then He saved the world through them.

Back to the hill...Even though Jesus died, the story wasn't over. Three days after dying on the cross, Jesus rose from His grave to prove that He is *still* alive. He had defeated death. He paid for sin, and then defeated death, which is the curse of sin. He did it all, just so we could be reconnected into a personal relationship with our Father, God. And now, thousands of years later, the legacy of Jesus who lived 33 years on our planet still reigns. He lived a sinless life, He paid the cost of our sin, and He became the bridge for you to a personal relationship with God. Even in your sin, your imperfection, you can know God. Because your sins have been paid for.

Here's a crazy thought. Thousands of years ago *you* were recognized. That's right. When Jesus hung on that cross, He paid the sin debt for mankind. That includes your specific debt. On that hill, Jesus recognized your need for a Savior and He took a step to rescue you from an eternity apart from God.

Do you remember what God cares most about in your life?

He cares most about your heart.

He knows that your heart is the wellspring of life (Proverbs 4:23). What God wants is for you to give Him your heart. He wants to connect with you on a heart level. He wants a relationship with Him. Since Jesus paid the price for our sins, He gave us access to God. Would you like to reconnect with God? You can just pray a simple prayer. (If you're worried about praying, don't be. God's not concerned about your words, He sees your heart. Even if you bumble through your words, He knows what you mean.)

But if you want a little direction, here's a prayer that you can pray:

"Lord Jesus, I need You. Thank You for dying on the cross in my place for my sins. I believe in You, I want to know You, and I want to have a relationship with You. Please come into my life and help me become the person that You

want me to be. Thank You for loving and rescuing me, God. I pray this in Jesus' name, amen."

Take a moment and pray if you want.

That, my friend, is amazing! One man named Jesus Christ changed this world forever. He now calls upon you and I to do the same in His name. Do you know Him? If so, does He drive how you impact your world? Your family? Your friends?

Jesus said that through Him life is abundantly found (John 10:10). I completely agree with that. Walking with God through life is an unbelievable adventure. It definitely isn't always easy, nowhere in the Bible does God promise an easy life for those who follow Him. But He does promise a fulfilling life!

My hope in writing this book is that you'd see another person that shares this planet with you who deals with the same stuff you do. I've done some pretty stupid things. I have some great struggles and as you can tell from reading about my life, I'm far from perfect. Life isn't perfect. People aren't perfect. Jesus changed the game. To put it in baseball terms, we were losing the game. He came out of the bullpen and saved the day. He saved the day for me and for you.

In a defining moment, Jesus once and for all recognized our sin and stepped in and paid a debt that we couldn't pay. You were part of this transaction. He paid your debt. He now offers you a life like no other. God loves you and I so much that He stepped in and rescued us. He wants us to know Him and to love Him so much.

I hope you'll be able to recognize God in your life. Friends and people will let you down. We will never be able to totally be perfect. But there are no limits on the One that gave His Son for us.

To finish up would you join me in asking God to help us see and know Him more? You can pray a prayer like this...

"God, thank You for the chance to stop and think about You. Help me to make a priority to do this more often, to simply stop and focus on You. Thank You for the journey that You have my life on, help me to always be learning from the ups and downs that You allow my life to take. Thank You for the greatest recognition ever— when Jesus

came to rescue me from my sin. Will You help me understand more and more every day how Your love and grace affects my life? Will You help me to follow You well, and be a positive difference in Your name in the lives of those You put in my life? May I be found fully in You. Thank You for Your love, Your grace, your freedom, and Your plan for my life. May the song of my life be to Your glory. I pray this in Jesus' name, amen."

It's quite simple. God is impressive. He is huge. I mean seriously huge. With modern technology we can now see more than 30 million light years from the earth. You know what? Our God has painted these amazing stars and galaxies. And just as much as He hung the stars, He made you. He knew you would one day walk this planet. He knows that your life is worth something—it's worth so much that He gave His Son's life to save it. He has put people in your life to help you to be the person He wants you to be, but your growth first starts by constantly being focused on Him.

My prayer for you is that on your journey of life that you will always make time to stop and acknowledge who God is and where you are. Next, I'm praying that you would take a moment and look back and learn from all that God is doing in and around you. I pray that you are reminded of the truth that not only did God recognize you many years ago at the cross, but also today He has you here for a reason. He knows you are here and He has an unbelievable plan for your life. He has given you freedom and charged you to be His ambassador to the world.

** If this is the first time that you have prayed that prayer…YES!!! You have just begun a personal relationship with our heavenly Father! I think this is the most important decision that you'll ever make. But, you can't do this alone! Go find someone that you know is a Christian and tell him or her about your newfound relationship in Him! Ask them to help you to grow in your faith! Congratulations!!!

The End

It's the last chapter! Yes! Congratulations on getting here! I really mean that, I know I've started a ton of books but haven't finished a lot of them. I do hope that this has been an engaging journey for you and I really appreciate you taking it with me.

On that note, we've set up a website, **www.jasoncarr.org**, where you'll be able to share any thoughts, feedback, and stories that you want to share after reading this. I promise you that I will read every one! If anything in the book has stirred up anything you want to share, go right ahead!

On a different note, I am notorious for being someone who likes to know what's going to happen. I'll admit, I'll sometimes go online and read up on movies or TV shows because I like to know what's going to happen. It sometimes drives my friends crazy because we can't have simple conversations about what we think might happen because the goober (me) has read ahead. I tend to ruin conversations about halfway through a season of *24*. I don't know why, but I love knowing what's going to happen. Some people can't even think about that, but that's how I am wired.

Here's something that I know for you: You have a choice to make today. No matter what your situation currently is, you have quite the journey in front of you. Only God truly knows how long, how far, and how much you have in your journey. It's our responsibility to trust and follow Him as we go. It's a tough choice to do that, to trust God with our journey. It would be easy to not trust Him and to try and do this thing on your own. I don't recommend that though because most of us who try that end up steering our lives in a direction that's quite far from what God intended our lives to be.

Walking with God takes a lot of guts. In many ways it's anti-cultural and definitely won't make things easy all the time. In fact, the Bible promises us that things are going to be tough. As Rocky Balboa said in the movie *Rocky Balboa:* "It's not about how hard you get hit, it's about how hard you can get hit and get up and keep fighting." I promise you that some hard blows are going to come your way.

Halt! Dismount And Be Recognized

I hope that you've read the truth that although some tough shots have been taken at me along my journey, God has been nothing but faithful. It's still pretty crazy to think about the fact that He still loves me. I'd have given up on me a long time ago, but He hasn't, and He hasn't given up on you either.

I've discovered that if I will take some time to stop, think about how faithful God has been and who I am in Him, I can fight through anything this world throws at me. I hope and pray that as you go live your journey that every now and then along the way you will halt, dismount, and be recognized.

I'm not a self-help guru trying to sell you some package for $19.99 that will make your life better. I'm just a very simple person whose life continues to be changed by an amazing God who has an undying love and desire for me to be the person He has put me here to be. It's by stopping, thinking about the past, and knowing who I am in God that makes me excited about whatever God has ahead for me.

Remember the roller coaster story from the introduction? No matter where you are at in your journey, you'll definitely have some high points and some low points coming. Plenty of twists and turns are on their way. The amazing thing is that your Creator will always be with you. I hope the truth of knowing that makes your journey incredible!

As we wrap up, please know that many people have been praying for you. We've been praying that you would walk away from your time here not just thinking about stories or stupid things that I've done, but about how much our heavenly Father truly loves you. We've prayed that God would use this to encourage and challenge you no matter where you are in your relationship with Him. I hope that has happened!

I think that all the days of our life we will be exploring this great collision of our everyday life and our incredible God. I hope that as you've had a chance to get a glimpse into my crazy world, you will walk away knowing the truth of how incredible our heavenly Father is. Only God knows what's in store with your journey, my friend. I hope as you travel along that you will take some time to stop, think about where you have been, and know where you are going.

Happy trails friends!

DIG DEEPER

Here are some songs that will help you connect a little more with "Be Recognized." As you listen to them, think about what you just read and how it connect from your ears to your heart.

"Love Song" from the Third Day CD *Third Day*
"Investigate" from the Delirious? CD *Glo*
"The Wonderful Cross" from the Chris Tomlin CD *The Noise We Make*
"Satisfy" from the Tenth Avenue North CD *Over and Underneath*
"Breathe on Me" from the North Point Live CD *Louder Than Creation*
"Beautiful the Blood" from the Fee CD *We Shine*
"Not Guilty Anymore" from the Aaron Keyes CD *Not Guilty Anymore*
"Bring You My Heart" from the Brett Younker CD *This Is Life*
"Movin' On" from the needtobreathe CD *The Heat*
"Sweetest Mystery" from the Eddie Kirkland CD *Orthodoxy*

Here are some verses to check out based on what you read:

Psalms 130:1-3, 13
Proverbs 3:5-6
John 10:10
John 16:33
Romans 3:23
Romans 6:23
1 Timothy 1:13-15

Here are some questions to help you think about what you just read:

- Where are the messages in your life coming from?
- Who do you think defines you are?

Halt! Dismount And Be Recognized

- What kind of "stuff" have you tried looking for your identity in?
- What are some messages in your life that you think you should question? Why?
- Why is it important to understand who you are?
- Whose choice do you think it is to define who you are?
- What does it mean to you to find your identity in Christ?
- How do you think we can know if we are "in Christ" or not?
- Did either of the prayers in the second-to-last chapter connect with you? Explain.
- This subtitle of the book you just read is this: "Exploring the collision of everyday life and an incredible God." Now that you've read the book, what does that mean to you?
- What has been your favorite part of the book? Why?
- What is something that you think God wants you to apply to your life or take with you as a result of reading this book?

The most important thing about who you are is what you think about God. I hope and pray that you will have the boldness and trust to talk to your friends about this last chapter. Find a safe place to ask any question on your heart!

As you've thought about your journey while reading this book, maybe someone else has come to mind. I think God has done that for a reason! Give them a call and go snag a cup of coffee with them and see what's going on in their life. You might just be the person God has in their life to help them get their journey back on track. (And hey, buying them a copy of the book would be great too!) Think about it, we're all on this journey of life together. Every one of us struggles with how we're recognized. If we don't place our faith and trust into a personal relationship with God, then we will likely turn our journey in a unwise direction. So, how will you be recognized?

It's a question that every person thinks about. The good news is that God has already answered it for you and I! Now it's our turn to choose how we want to be recognized...happy trails! Enjoy the journey!

.thank You.

In most books the "thank you" page is found in the front. I wanted to put these towards the back because the names and people on this page represent so much of what you just read.

George; I was serious about what I said way back that day a few years ago at Dreamland, thanks. You have believed in me so much-there has been many times when your belief and encouragement in me has kept me going. Your kindness, friendship, and faith in who God has called me to be has been nothing short of a gift from our Heavenly Father.

All my friends and co-workers from my season at North Point: Kevin, Shef, Marcelo, Clint, Ashley, Donny, Phillip, Ryan, Sara, Sarah, Liz, Cara, Caroline, Britt, Kelly, Ben, Drew, Julie, Clay, Jennifer, Beth, John, KT and Jayce. You are all doing things that will last for eternity!

Thanks to the Student Venture ministry for giving me the opportunity and responsibility that you did. It was quite the journey wasn't it? I'm grateful for all that you do. You are fighting a great battle on the front lines! Special thanks to Mike and Warren for all you've done for me. I've learned so much from you and will always be thankful for your influence on my life.

Terry: What can I say? God has used you in ways I can never express. I am grateful God has a big enough sense of humor to put you in my life. God has used you to shape me in so many ways. We are like dynamite together. Keep 'em straight and fire it up my friend…did you smell something?

Laurin: Thanks for your hard work making this read much better than I write. I can't explain how grateful I am that you took this project on. You're the best!

Jo: One day people are going to see this and think, "Jo designed that? Wow, Jason sure was lucky!" And they are right, I am. Thanks Jo!

A big thanks to: Darren Youngstrom, Joe Thibodeau. Clete Terrell and the ever-changing "Back Porch Gang" for the hours of pontification, soul shaping and world problem solving. You guys have been such an important part of my journey- thanks.

Tom and Elaine: Your belief in me over the years has been simply humbling. It has meant more than you will ever know. Thank you for everything!

To all of my faithful ministry partners over the years, you give me the ability to do what I do. I hope that you have been continually encouraged by what God is doing.

Randy and Terri: Your generosity made a huge difference in getting this moving and then done. The cabin is a Godsend and the timing was nothing less than perfect- it refilled my tank (twice!). Thanks.

Nancy and Barry: Thanks for harboring the Murph and I for a while. I will always be grateful for the incredible generosity that you have shown me.

Thanks to: Justin and Rachel Land, Matt and Rachel Melton, Matt and Beth Dashner, Rob and Becca Attaway, Pat Malone (and the "coffee shop" club), Glenn and Jill Archer, Abbie Smith, Sean and Beth Pitts, Todd and Mia Crane, Jason and Rachel Brubaker, Mark and Jami Gilliam, Starbucks Coffee, Danny and Vicki Dukes, Chuck Pitts, Jeff and Cinnamon and family, Kings Ridge Christian School and all the various churches and ministries I've had the opportunity to be a part of!

To Lanny Donoho, John Smoltz, and Reggie Joiner: thanks for the incredibly kind words. I'm honored.

For everyone who has prayed and supported this dream- thanks! If I had a dollar for every time one of you asked me when this would be done I would be a wealthy man. Thanks for caring and praying, it's meant so much.

Mom and Dad…you have always supported me! You have encouraged me whether I was playing football, playing music, going off to college, working with SV, on the run all over the place, and whatever crazy direction my life has gone. I could never express what you mean to me. Please know that I sincerely love you. Thank you for allowing me the freedom to chase my dreams and the grace to open your door when they sometimes crash. I seem to have a habit of taking for granted too often how special a gift you are to me. Thank you for always being there. The biggest impression you have given me is your constant love and support…I love you and hope to one-day be like you guys in the lives of others. You two are a model to the world of what it means to love others as Christ loves us. Thank you for the example you are!

My Daddy, Father, Abba…God. You know. You have been "it" for a long time. You really are my closest and best friend I have in this world. You constantly sweep me away to a place of grace and peace. You have never left me or forsaken me. You are always by my side. I am yours…these words are here for You to use how You choose…have Your own way. May these words give You what You deserve and the impression be made of You and You alone.

About The Author

Jason Carr currently serves on the student ministry staff at North Point Community Church in Alpharetta, Ga. (www.northpoint.org.) Jason's hobbies include reading, writing, spending time with friends, a great cup of coffee, movies, pounce, sports and music. He spends his free time investing in students, leaders, and community ministries while single handedly keeping Starbucks open.

Jason has also written leaders guides and music reviews for YouthWalk magazine. (www.ywspace.org)

Jason currently lives in his hometown of Alpharetta, GA. He is the proud owner of Murphy, a hyperactive golden retriever.

For more information about Jason, please visit his web site at **www.jasoncarr.org**.

Book cover designed by Jo Albright.

You can contact Jo here:
www.joalbright.wordpress.com

Printed in the United States
203637BV00004B/199-1176/P